Brain-sav

C000175540

How wom
overcome gender bias
and succeed at work

First published by Head Heart + Brain 2017

4 Vivian Road London E3 5RF

www.headheartbrain.com

info@hhab.co.uk

British Library Cataloguing in Publication Data

A CIP catalogue record for this book is available from the British library

ISBN 978-0-9929007-6-2

Also by Jan Hills:

Brain-Savvy HR: A neuroscience evidence base 2014

Brain-Savvy Business: 8 principles for neuroscience and how to apply them 2016

There's heaps in this book that resonates and that challenges me - as a woman, a mother, a colleague, a leader and a people specialist. A fascinating read for everyone who wants to deepen their understanding of the dangers of stereotypes and to find practical ways to move beyond them.

Caroline Rawes
Chief People Officer, Ashurst

An interesting new approach to gender bias: mother and daughter team Jan and Francesca Hills highlight how entrenched discrimination still is in the work place. The great thing about this book is that is provides tools and guidance to help you address the challenges this brings. Interestingly many of these techniques are very simple, like language and body posture, but they will help women to achieve their ambitions and get the positions and pay that they deserve.

This book is essential reading for ambitious women – and all leaders who want to create a more inclusive workplace.

Lynda Tyler
Non-Executive Director and advisor to CEOs,
Founder and Principal Tyler Cagni Consulting Ltd

A man endorsing a book that talks about inclusion of women might seem odd, but gender equality is simply the first horizon in the journey to inclusiveness. There are new horizons beyond that, and I encourage everyone to read from both ends of this book because in truth we are each a minority of one, and regardless of what makes that so, we can all benefit from the very practical lessons in overcoming bias that are covered here.

David Perks
CEO and Founder, Pay Compliment

Retaining and developing diverse talent will always be key to long-term business success. This book, with the meticulous research we have come to expect from Head, Heart + Brain, is a powerful guide to how to realise your own potential, and the potential of your organisation, regardless of your career stage.

Ben Fletcher
Managing Director for UK and Europe, Clarks

At a time when there is so much frustration about the persistent lack of progress in creating gender balance in organisations, Brain-Savvy Wo+man provides a rich combination of neurobiological and psychological insights and practical strategies for creating more sustainable, fulfilling and successful careers.

Jane Lewis
Director of People and Culture, Allens LLP

The differential perceptions of the make-up of women and men has been analysed in search of gender enlightenment for some considerable time. But only now are the implications for business being explored in earnest. At a time of heightened interest in gender fluidity, Francesca and Jan Hills' work constitutes an invaluable and timely primer for both women and men navigating their careers through waters that are only now beginning to be charted.

Ed Warner OBE
Chair, Grant Thornton UK

Thank you

When you conceive of a book in back-to-back halves, it's hard to know where to place the thanks which apply to the whole project. The middle seemed the logical place but no one will ever see it! So, it's here but of course our thanks apply to both ends of the book.

Every publishing project is a creative adventure that requires a whole lot of enthusiasm and support to come to fruition. As a mother-and-daughter writing team we need to start by thanking each other for all the extra discipline, flexibility and patience that's been necessary to get this project all the way to print, with our relationship intact. We have not only lived to tell the tale – we've had fun. And we now have even more respect for each other. Enough said.

Since this is a book about career development, purpose and inspiration, we have naturally been thinking about the people who have been instrumental in our own careers. Jan knows that she wouldn't be running her own consultancy without wonderful clients who have let her use these ideas in their organisations. And the female support of her Brilliant Women dinner group: Sam, Helen, Elaine, Morag, Lindsay, Sarah, Sian, Mel, Caroline and Nicole.

Francesca wants to thank her team who have been so enthusiastic about the book project, and her mentor, colleagues and clients who have helped her grow and flourish. And, most of all, her close friendship group who have been a huge support this year.

We are indebted to Jan's longstanding colleagues at Head Heart + Brain, Lindsay Hanson and Sarah North, who compiled the Exploring Further content, read the difficult chapters we were stuck on, and came up with the idea of using our clients' own career challenges to introduce the content. We couldn't have completed the book without their commitment and insightful analysis. They will be bringing their expertise to the women's career development programme that is based on this book – a new venture for Head Heart + Brain that we're all excited about.

And of course we want to thank all those people who agreed to be interviewed, or completed the survey. It's extraordinarily generous of these busy people to give their time, and many of them told us that they were willing to be involved because they felt the issues were so important.

We have been fortunate to work again with an enthusiastic and tirelessly professional book publishing team. Our editor Jennifer Stevenson was able to climb inside the concept of this book, offering structural suggestions as well as turning our text into lucid and engaging prose. There were a few "gin-and-tonic" chapters (as in "you'll need a gin and tonic as you read the comments on this version") but we survived them. You can tell how good she is: she drafted this paragraph. She's incredibly cheeky but we have had lots of laughs along the way.

Then there's our creative and endlessly patient designer Dougal Burgess. This is the third book he has designed in the Brain-Savvy series and his clean but quirky style suits our subject-matter so well. Instead of throwing his hands up in horror he embraced the slightly mad idea of a double-ended book as an interesting design challenge. He also worked long nights to get it designed on time and for that we are especially grateful. We'll miss the late night calls!

And thanks to Bill Porter, our illustrator. We love his illustrations and think they work with our content; we feel he excelled himself on this book.

And finally, how fortunate we were to also have an eagle-eyed proof-reader in the family: Francesca's brother, Elliott Hills. He went through the final manuscript and the proofs with the proverbial fine tooth-comb (does anyone still comb their teeth these days?). He was both meticulous and insightful, making suggestions "out of scope" which enhanced the final text. Thank you, Elliott.

Contents

less committed? / Self-fulfilling stereotypes / Pick your moments of super-competence / Mindfulness to trigger change / What image do you project? / Show potential as much as achievements

12. Own your ambition p.221

Jay is tipped for higher management; has Meena been "passed over"? / Can you be feminine and ambitious? / Opting out... or redefining / Mastery requires recognition / Women at the centre of their own success / The family dilemma / Allocating personal resources / Challenges to ambition / Closing the gap / Build your own support network / Find mentors and sponsors / Imagine your future

13. Why women *still* have to perform better than men p.237

Jay is interviewed for a directorship; why isn't Meena visible? / The double standards / Micro messages and micro-responses / Prove it again... and again / More experience needed for pay increases and promotion / Proving commitment / Skills assumptions / More rigorous criteria / "High rewards could make the men jealous" / Penalties for women's flexible working / Tactics to challenge double standards

14. Resisting the backlash against strong women p.257

Is Meena too confrontational? Jay tells her what the male directors think / Recognise this scenario? / Penalties of challenging the hierarchy / Awareness alone doesn't change behaviour / Stepping outside normal / How to stand up to the onslaught / Challenging

1.
Why you need this book

This half of the book takes a specifically female perspective on managing your career. Old-fashioned workplaces that are directed by tired old stereotypes no longer suit how either men or women want or expect to work today, but we can't ignore the fact that most of the changes need to happen to improve things for women.

The gender biases and double standards that still persist in our organisations *do* have more of an impact for women. There *is* a gender pay gap. Women still struggle to get recognition of their skills and are slower to be promoted and still struggle to reach their place at the top of organisations. We can't ignore that men *do* have a disproportionate hold on the positions of power and influence, and still sit in 84% of the seats on executive committees in the top 350 UK businesses.

But because this is a book that focuses on neurological and psychological insights, rather than political campaigning, we'll be looking at how the beliefs about women and their confidence and competence (or myths, or partial truths) that frame our reality, stack up against the research. And we'll look at the practical steps we ourselves can take to address the current beliefs.

What... still?

Now if you just read that and you're thinking, "*Is* there still entrenched inequality?" you're in good company. In a survey conducted for this book by co-author Jan's leadership consultancy Head Heart + Brain, we had responses from over 1,000 people (two-thirds of them women) and interviewed leaders in around 30 organisations across the globe. Nearly 70% of women in the survey said they hadn't experienced any discrimination at work.

And that's great, of course. But that leaves around 30% who have.

So, if you don't believe you've been treated differently because of your gender, think of this as an interesting book that might have some useful insights and tools for managing your career, and skip the science on gender bias and stereotypes. Though that content might prove useful if you move into a leadership role in another organisation and you realise you need to make some changes there.

But please don't assume that if it hasn't happened to you it doesn't happen at all.

If you're in the 30% that has experienced discrimination (and many of the women we surveyed only became aware of how it might be working against them once they had been working for 10 to 15 years) this book can help you. You'll find out more about what bias looks like, why it happens, and what to do about it with practical tools, tips and smooth comebacks.

Our perspective on the challenges for women

Much of the writing about gender subtly (and sometimes not-so-subtly) blames women. Women just need to change to be successful in a (male) world.

That's not our view. We do think that forewarned is forearmed and tooled-up is sensible. But we also want to see workplaces changed for the better, so that it's not always down to individual women to adapt for survival. And our aim is to help you to become the kind of leaders who will be at the forefront of those changes.

This book is designed to equip you to thrive in the workplace whatever your experience: from no bias (or at least none that you've noticed) to outright discrimination that means you're never going to get to where you want without action.

And because your authors are both women – we are mother and daughter: a leadership and business consultant and an account executive for a strategic media company – we are both personally as well as professionally concerned with how women face different challenges at work. We may face many of the same issues as men, but women experience them, and tackle them, in different ways.

Our belief is that improving the workplace for women improves it for everyone. And we know from the research that unless you are a stereotypical aggressive, driven man you too will be affected by bias. So, you might also find this half of the book of interest: dip in and see.

Meet the people

For each chapter, in both halves of the book, we've used the experiences of both a man and a woman who raise the challenges they're facing, as a way of unwrapping the scientific evidence and then providing the strategies and tools to address their challenges. To spare their blushes and save their careers, they are an amalgam of people we've worked with, at different points in their careers.

We are all biased

Nobel laureate psychologist and founder of behavioural economics Daniel Kahneman demonstrated that what he calls the "System 1" part of the brain works automatically, without effort and control. According to Columbia neuroscientist Eric Kandel, who has also worked in the field of the unconscious mind, our unconscious accounts for 80-90% of how our mind works. This is bias at its most basic.

It's not all bad: as a default mechanism these unconscious processes help us to deal with masses of data and make decisions quickly. But they also mean we are vulnerable to acting and making decisions without realising we are being influenced by unconscious implicit associations – some of which result in gender bias.

Without knowing it, we spend years learning stereotypes which become the foundations of our prejudices – our biased thinking. The first step is to realise that this can be a problem. Unfortunately, that isn't always easy. We're all happy to believe that other people may be biased, but we resist any suggestion that we may be biased ourselves. So it's not surprising that it's so difficult to identify positive results from "diversity training." (And some researchers are beginning to suggest that such training can actually be counterproductive.)

Understanding the reality of gender bias

Many women believe they haven't been affected by gender bias at work. And that may be the case, or it may be that we have been so conditioned to accept the status quo that we genuinely don't notice the language, the assumptions and the micro-inequalities; we've become gender-bias blind.

And it's even less likely that men will be aware of bias: it typically works in their favour and they're desensitised to see it.

But the figures don't lie. The gender pay gap: in the UK women earn 80p for every £1 that men earn. The unequal numbers of women in leadership: only 35% of women have profit-and-loss roles in the top 350 UK companies)

Extensive research shows there is no fundamental biological difference which makes women less able at maths, technical jobs or leadership roles, and plenty of evidence that we are all socialised to behave in particular ways and expect particular behaviours, and to punish (socially) anyone who doesn't comply with our expectations. ("Wow – you've only taken six months' maternity leave? It must be hard for you to leave your tiny baby in the care of strangers...")

We wrote this book to broaden both men and women's understanding: to lay out the myths and share the latest evidence of the practices and behaviours which will help you counteract gender bias. This half of the book is written specifically for women, but many men will find the information interesting and all the tools can be equally useful in dealing with the challenges and stereotypes men must manage. (Not all men are treated equally.)

Whether you feel you've been disadvantaged or you have genuinely never been affected by the issues, you will find ideas on how to manage your career and become the kind of leader who will create the progressive gender-neutral organisations of the future.

Male and female brains – how different are they?

Some titles from the gender-aware office library bookshelf:

Men Are from Mars, Women Are from Venus

Play Like a Man, Win Like a Woman: What Men Know
About Success that Women Need to Learn

The X and Y of Leadership: How Men and Women Make a
Difference at Work

The Loudest Duck: Moving Beyond Diversity While
Embracing Differences to Achieve Success at Work

Whenever we talk with a group about neuroscience, we inevitably get the question: are there differences between men and women's brains. The short answer: there are some, possibly. The more complex question is: do they decide how people will always behave at work, and are there other, more important factors at play?

Physical differences between men's and women's brains

This is a thorny issue and we thought it would be useful to summarise the current understanding.

Israeli research has shown that distinctive differences between male and female brains can be seen in the womb as early as 26 weeks. Researchers at the University of California-Irvine have found that men have 6.5 times more grey matter than women; sometimes called "thinking matter" it makes up the brain's information-processing centres. Women's brains have 9.5 times more of the interconnecting white matter which connects these processing centres. "Female brains might be more efficient," says Richard Haier, lead psychologist on the study.

Patterns of connectivity

A study by Dr Ragini Verma of the University of Pennsylvania looked at the connections in the cerebrum, which is above and towards the front of the brain (and responsible for activities like thinking), and the cerebellum below and towards the back of the brain (that's responsible for taking action).

Each of these brain areas is divided into two hemispheres: the right and left sides of the brain. In the cerebrum, male brains are more connected *within* the hemispheres, in females across the hemispheres. And in the cerebellum the differences are the other way around (male brains are more connected *across* the hemispheres). Verma believes this reflects the cognitive skill differences between men and women which we discuss further below.

Size: does it matter?

One argument that has historically been used to explain differences in male and female capabilities is size. The brain in human males is on average about 10% larger than female brains. But although the extra mass potentially give males more processing-power, it doesn't necessarily mean that it's used, or that men use it to be more intelligent.

Most scientists believe that the difference in size can be accounted for by the need to operate a larger male body mass (men's bodies are on average 15-20% larger than women's). Women perform just as well as men in intelligence tests (if you believe IQ tests measure anything reliable).

200 year-old prejudices

You might have read that these differences in physical structure and size account for why men and women seem to be better at different things. Two hundred years ago author and clergyman Thomas Gisborne wrote: "The science of legislation, of jurisprudence, of political economy, the conduct of government... these and other studies...assigned chiefly or entirely to men demand the efforts of mind eluded with the powers of close and comprehensive reasoning and of intense application."

We can only hope that all women have had the good fortune to work for men of such undisputed mental superiority as this!

According to Gisborne these qualities had been given to females with a "sparing hand" because they had less need of them. His argument was that women are just different and when it comes to performance in the female sphere "the superiority of the female mind is unrivalled." Women, he claims, have powers "adapted to unbend the brow of the learned, to refresh the over-laboured faculties of the wise..." (so get to it, girls!).

Science moves on... slowly

And it might appear that science had discovered little to refute this. As late as 2004, when a Cambridge psychologist Simon Baron-Cohen tells us in his book the *Essential Difference*: "The female brain is predominately hard wired for empathy. The male brain is predominately hard wired for understanding and building systems."

It would be easy to think these differences explain why working women have clustered in "the caring professions" and men in other careers, why we still struggle to get enough women and girls into sciences and maths, and why women's leadership is said to focus around relationships and empathy.

Essentially Gisborne's assigned roles have become the prevailing beliefs about male and female abilities. And brain science (including psychology and neuroscience) has focused on trying to prove or disprove these beliefs. It will be apparent as you read on that many of the so-called scientific investigations are little more than efforts to prove the authors' own prejudices, and may still be influencing how researchers interpret the latest scientific techniques such as neuroscience's exciting toy: real-time functional magnetic resonance imaging (fMRI scans).

Do the differences make men or women smarter / faster / better?

Let's discuss some of the common differences attributed to male and female brains and their apparent impact on performance.

Men tend to process more in the left side of their brains, women tend to use both left and right-sides.

Brain volume and ability

"Females seem to have language functioning in both sides of the brain," according to Martha Bridge Denckla of the Kennedy Krieger Institute. And this activity across both hemispheres is thought to promote stronger intuition, and women's better language and verbal communication skills.

Evolutionary psychologist David Geary maintains that if there is a greater brain area dedicated to a set of skills, it follows that the skills will be more refined. "The frontal area of the cortex and the temporal area of the cortex are more precisely organised in women, and are bigger in volume," says Geary. Again, this difference may go towards explaining the apparent advantage women have in language skills .

Differential language skills

It appears that men are more likely to use a small area of the brain, on just one side, for a particular task; women typically use more of the brain, in both hemispheres, for the same task. And the evolutionary hypothesis for this is that women needed language and emotional skills to manage important tribal relationships with their peers, and their children, while the men were away hunting.

Geary suggests that this behaviour, referred to as "relational aggression" may have given females a survival advantage long ago. "If the ability to use language to organise relationships was of benefit during evolutionary history, and used more frequently by women, we would expect language differences to become exaggerated," he says.

Studies show that women use language to build relationships today. "Women pause more, allow the other person to speak more, offer facilitative gestures," Geary says. Women use this to their advantage, he suggests: "Females use language more when they compete. They gossip, manipulate information." Many women might not acknowledge the benefits of gossip, but... information is power.

Multi-tasking and map-reading (that old chestnut...)

Another perceived difference between the genders is in tasks that involve spatial navigation, which men are generally believed to be better at than women. The differences in "wiring" referred to earlier may explain why men, whose brains are mainly connected within the hemispheres, can focus on tasks that don't need input from both hemispheres.

Hence the belief that men find multitasking more difficult and tend to focus on one thing at a time. In the cerebellum, the cross-hemisphere links related to action gives men better motor abilities and physical coordination.

Map-reading abilities are a perennial favourite in the gender-difference debate. Women, it transpires, are more likely to rely on landmark cues for direction ("*Turn right at the Fox and Goose pub*") while men are more likely to use abstract concepts ("*Go east for a mile*").

Those different strategies correlate with different brain regions. Neuroscientists have found that women use the cerebral cortex (mostly the right parietal cortex) while men use primarily the left hippocampus, a nucleus deep inside the brain which remains inactive in women's brains during navigational tasks. Both methods of navigation patently work (there's no evidence of thousands of women roaming the roads every day, unable to find their destinations) but they are very different, as are the brain areas involved.

Nature or nurture

One theory is that their different spatial abilities served men well while they were hunting. An alternative view is that nurture develops these differences in children. Martha Bridge Denckla claims there is persuasive evidence that we build up our brain's representation of space by moving through space. And anyone who spends time around children knows that boys tend to get a lot more practice "moving through space" (chasing balls, for instance) than girls do.

She believes that we could possibly erase this difference if girls were actively encouraged at a young age to do more physical games requiring co-ordination. She predicts that as more and more girls engage in sports traditionally reserved for boys the data on spatial ability will show fewer disparities.

Men don't "do" emotions?

Neuroscientists at Harvard have used fMRI imaging to study how emotion is processed in the brains of children between the ages of 7 and 17. They found that emotional activity was localised in primitive subcortical areas of the brain, specifically in the amygdala.

That's one reason why most 6-year-olds cannot tell you why they are feeling sad: the part of the brain that does the talking, the cerebral cortex, doesn't connect to the part of the brain where the emotion is occurring, the amygdala, until much later in life. In adolescence, brain activity associated with emotion moves up to the cerebral cortex. The 17-year-old is able to explain what she is feeling, and why.

But that change occurs only in girls. In boys, the locus of emotional control remains in the amygdala, which may be why some adolescent boys find it hard to talk about emotions – and for some that continues into adulthood.

Fight / flight or tend & befriend

Women, on the whole, are also perceived to be better than men at managing their emotions. Researchers have recently discovered that sections of the brain used to control aggression and anger responses are larger in women than in men. And there is evidence that in stressful events men are more likely to adopt the fight / flight response while women favour "tend and befriend."

And Cambridge neuroscientist John Coates claims that men and women tend to be stressed by different issues: while women have the same levels of stress hormones as men, they're generally triggered by social rather than competitive stress. Like arguing amongst the team for women, and competition to bring in the highest revenue for men.

But our brains are also very similar...

Studying differences is very interesting, but male and female brains share a multiplicity of structures and functions, and are more similar than they are different. And studies in neuroplasticity suggest that nurturing and training the brain offers exciting possibilities for enhancing what nature has provided.

A series of studies has found that women indeed do appear better at language and relational skills *but only* when they are primed to be like that. Nancy Eisenberg and Randy Lennon reviewed studies on gender differences in empathy and found that women showed less advantage in empathy when it was not obvious that it was being tested. In other, primed, research (that is, when it was suggested that empathy was important), men were just as able to be empathetic as women.

And similar results have been found on maths tests and on spatial tests. ("If it's important, I'll be good at it!")

Living up to the stereotypes

In other words, women – and men – live up to the stereotypes expected of them by society. And these sorts of results suggest that stereotypes are mainly responsible for the gender-based differences which are so pervasive in society and business.

If you're rather dismayed by this as a woman, feeling that your empathetic advantage has been eroded, consider the other side of the coin: you and your daughters are just as capable of doing anything a man can. There is nothing biological holding back your maths or science understanding, and you can problem-solve and strategise, read maps and give directions as well as any man if you so desire (as many women know).

And a man can be just as good at empathy and "talking about things" when the stereotypes don't hold sway. Much of the rest of this half of the book will help you to understand the stereotypes and how to overcome them if you want to.

Dodging the stereotypes

We can see how it's possible to dodge the stereotypes when we look at studies which trick the mind into thinking it is the opposite gender. Participants in a series of experiments by Adam Galinsky at Northwestern University were asked to write about a day in the life a professor, an elderly man, an African American man or a cheerleader; they were asked to imagine they were the person and to write about their day in the first person ("I woke up and saw it was a lovely day...").

Afterwards participants were asked to rate their own personal traits and it was found that they rated themselves higher on traits associated with the stereotype they had been imagining. Those who had written about the professor rated themselves as more analytical, whilst those who walked in the shoes of the cheerleader rated themselves a more attractive and sexy.

The re-imagining also impacted behaviour. Women who took the perspective of the professor for the day did better on analytical tests than control participants, while those who had "been" the cheerleader performed worse. The stereotypical characteristics were incorporated into the participants' self-concepts and this influenced their abilities.

What are the implications at work?

The debate about male and female strengths and preferences continues, as do discussions about whether scientist who "prove" there are differences are really being led by their own preconceptions. There's no evidence that the measurable differences favour one gender over the other at work. But they do make it clear how powerful stereotypes can be, and how they shape our behaviour.

More on that, and how we can work within those constraints, and change them, in later chapters.

Exploring further

Books

Delusions of Gender: How Our Minds, Society, and Neurosexism Create Difference, Cordelia Fine (Debunks some of the popular myths about apparent differences in the brain and gender, and the books written around them.)

Articles, blogs and podcasts

Educate everyone about second generation gender bias, Herminia Ibarra, Robin J. Ely, and Deborah Kolb (Second generation gender bias is embedded in stereotypes and hence invisible to many women.) HBR

Videos and webinars

Movies' View of Women is Unbalanced, Geena Davis (The Academy Award-winning actor talks about the perception of women in the media and what has – and hasn't – changed in the past 60 years.) Wall Street Journal (4: 49)

The missing piece in the gender equality puzzle, Joselyn DiPetta (Trying to increase social, economic, and political equality for women by focusing on women is an ineffective strategy says this organisational trainer.) TEDx (17: 33)

Body language and gender from a dancer's perspective, Natalia Khosla (As a senior at Yale studying psychology and dance Khosla questions the relationship between body language and our perceptions of gender.) TEDx (13: 05)

Honest Liars – The Psychology of Self-Deception, Cortney Warren (A thought-provoking talk about the need to be self-aware and honest with ourselves.) TEDx (13: 48)

Other resources

Leanin.org (Lots of resources, articles and videos on gender in the workplace.)

2.
Warning: sex stereotypes at work

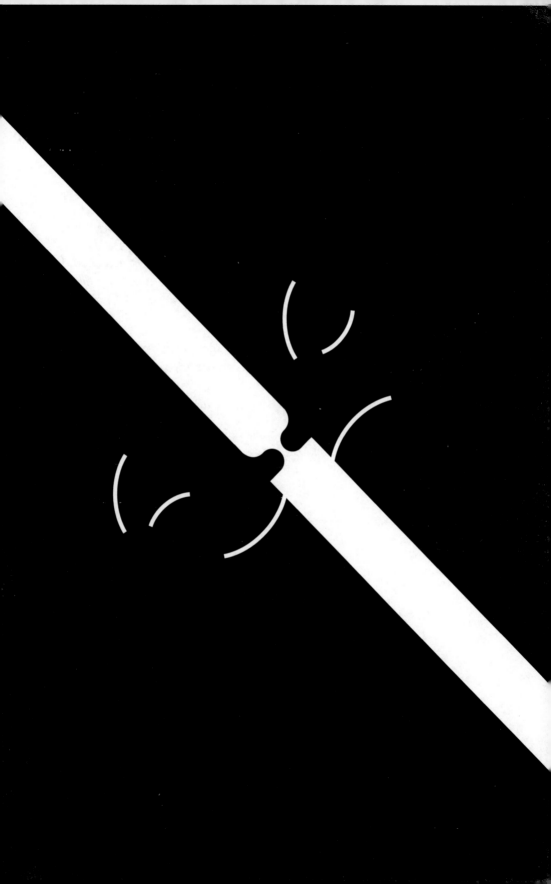

Siobhan and Nikhil are graduate recruits who've become friends sharing experiences in their first year at Multinational Trading Plc, a major technical services organisation. They've survived "bluffing through" their first hectic months, learning the ropes and figuring out the relationships in their teams. They're just beginning to feel they're not completely useless.

Nikhil has observed that the guys whose work gets noticed are fairly brash and self-promoting. It's not his style, and he doesn't quite feel like "one of the lads." He wonders if he needs to be more opinionated and assertive.

Siobhan is well aware of the laddish guys Nikhil has to contend with, but feels she has bigger problems that don't affect him. Her boss keeps asking her to get the coffee in meetings. At first she was pleased to have a role, but she notices he never asks the guys. The women in her department hardly say anything in meetings, especially if the client is there. Siobhan is still trying to work out the rules. Should she speak up, and say something about the coffee?

It's not surprising that Siobhan and Nikhil are shocked and disappointed to find that sex bias is still alive and raising its overbearing voice in workplaces the length and breadth of the country. Many young women in particular would like to believe that gender bias is over-hyped.

You may need to be convinced, so let's just quickly cover the basics of what gender bias *is*, what does it look like at work, what's the evidence that it still persists, and if it is still around... why is it so difficult to root out?

What our clients tell us

The Gender in the Workplace survey carried out by author Jan Hills' Head Heart + Brain consultancy surveyed the work experiences of just over 1,000 men and women aged from 16 to 70 in a range of organisations and industries around the world. The responses included this comment from a 47 year-old woman who runs a business unit in the pharmaceutical industry: "Unsurprisingly, women do not do well where the subjective nature of potential is evaluated by male-dominated groups who just don't see women as 'young versions of themselves.'"

And a 28 year-old man told us that what is needed to stop gender bias is: "Role-modelling from senior officials, feminist allies to call out sexist behaviour, and reverse mentoring from younger staff members of the opposite gender."

Sex stereotypes: surviving and kicking

More than 40 years after the UK's ground-breaking Sex Discrimination Act came into law, this feels like it should be yesterday's battle: one that a previous generation of feminists have fought and won.

There *are* now women heading up the UK's FTSE 100 companies – though only seven of them (in 2017). As is so depressingly pointed out, there are still twice as many men named John who are CEOs or chairmen of FTSE 100s as there are women of any name. There *are* women priests (though not bishops), and surgeons, and heads of government departments, and CEOs of charities, and prime ministers – though not presidents of the US.

It's no longer acceptable for leaders to suggest that women are out of place at work, or that they just don't have the chops to make it to the top. Witness the furore when self-confessed chauvinist Nobel prize-winning biochemist Sir Tim Hunt said in 2015 that women in science labs were a distraction, and tended to burst into tears. He resigned after the devastatingly effective (and hilariously funny) #DistractinglySexy twitterstorm by senior women scientists.

But it's still an uphill battle. It's still easy to undermine progressive action with accusations of "political correctness". (Boris Johnson, then Mayor of London, said the response to Tim Hunt's comments had been an "overreaction" and it was not wrong to point out "gender differences".) And all of this is because of the persistence of workplace stereotypes, we argue.

What is a "stereotype"?

We define a stereotype as a cognitive "shortcut" that categorises people based on characteristics such as gender, race, or age. They are a type of bias which is a semi-permanent belief formed by repeated exposure to pictures or connections made between, for example, people and places, or people and situations. We unconsciously memorise the association, creating the stereotype in our minds.

What Siobhan and Nikhil have come up against are deeply ingrained stereotypes of how people at work (and in most social situations) are expected to behave. Stereotypes come with a whole host of assumptions, and when those assumptions are challenged they cause people to behave in a way designed to keep the belief in place. Research has found people will filter information, find excuses and even deny their own observations rather than change their stereotypical belief.

It's this attempt to keep the stereotypes in place, to maintain the beliefs which result in explicit discrimination, implicit bias and other behaviour which treats women in a different (and usually unbeneficial) way to men.

What workplace stereotypes look like

For example, men at work, especially men in senior positions, are expected to have a strong point of view and an authoritative (some would say forceful, or aggressive) way of expressing it. They're expected to be strategic and to be willing to take risks. Men who don't exhibit these characteristics may be thought of as "lacking drive," and "not forceful enough" to be leadership material.

Women, by contrast, are expected to be collaborative and concerned about relationships, and focused on the team achieving things collectively rather than individual achievements. If they press their point of view, or are unapologetic about their personal ambition they may be seen as "pushy", "overbearing" and "not a team player."

Do you recognise this behaviour?

Because, historically, men have held senior roles, especially the senior technical roles, women are still mistaken for the assistant. In our

Gender in the Workplace survey people reported numerous examples: team members assuming that a female engineer must be the wife of a colleague; the trainer saying how good it was that the secretary could sit in on a managerial course. Automatically describing a leader as "he". Yes, in 2017; the examples would be funny except that even comedy writers wouldn't try to get laughs out of such tired old material.

Would you automatically get up to help a male colleague pass coffees around the conference table? Or have you ever been caught out in an automatic assumption that a CEO is a man? No-one will comment on the former. The latter might trigger an awkward "whoops!" – but only if the CEO is actually a woman. If the CEO is a man, the automatic assumption usually passes completely unremarked.

Stereotypes are so pervasive, and their influence so pernicious, that it's important to understand how they work and why they persist long after they have ceased to be "acceptable."

How stereotypes are created

Consider this short account of someone recounting their journey to work this morning:

> *The argument with the head of technology was still on my mind when I found myself slamming on the brakes in my car to avoid a collision: a driver had stopped with no warning to drop off their child, just in front of me. I was still shaking as I carried on to deliver my screaming child with the childminder. It was a stressful morning and it had barely started.*

Now quickly look at the images you've had in your mind's eye:

- Was the head of technology a male?
- Was the bad driver female?
- Was the narrator female? And the childminder?

This is implicit bias and it's hardly surprising, considering how embedded it is even in online media. A Google search for "doctor" + "images" returns 75% male pictures (just over half the GPs in the UK are women).

These stereotypes are the result of how our brains work. Nobel award-winning psychologist Daniel Kahneman described the two styles of processing in the brain as System 1 and System 2: System 1 uses mental shortcuts to process vast amounts of data before engaging System 2, our slower, rational brain.

Life is fast, we need to work quickly; when we're making decisions our quick-thinking System 1 often jumps to conclusions without checking in with the rational System 2. A quick decision can be helpful but it can be based on assumptions that are outdated. That's what sustains gender bias, and just being aware of it won't change it. You need to create a conscious intention to check your decisions, or have someone else who thinks differently help you to do that.

Early conditioning: boys take up more space

Our stereotypes are deeply ingrained because they're imprinted early. For example: Harvard Business School psychologist Amy Cuddy, who is currently studying body language, has observed that men are more likely to use expansive postures and open gestures. In the workplace these gestures – taking up room, using wide arm gestures, standing with legs spread – are associated with confidence and have become associated with masculine leaders.

Amy Cuddy's research identifies the age at which children start to associate expansive posture with males and contractive posture with females. It's very young: around four years old. Cuddy has shown that children believe that wooden dolls in expansive postures are boys and that wooden dolls in contractive postures are girls. And a documentary series *The Secret Life of 5 Year Olds* revealed how children already had fixed ideas of male and female behaviour, capabilities and roles. (At the end of this chapter you'll find details of a trailer for the series in which one little girl is a striking exception.)

The brain loves to categorise

Whenever we encounter someone for the first time we automatically categorise them into a mental in-group (of people we see as being like ourselves) or an out-group (the people who are somehow different from us). This categorisation can take as little as 30milliseconds and happens totally outside of conscious thought – in fact before we have even consciously registered anything about the person.

Once the categorisation is made we react positively to our in-group and are less well-disposed to the out-group, and this response, which was protective in early evolution, is problematic in modern organisational culture. We tend to objectify the out-group and over-empathise with our in-group. And the associated features of the numerous sub-categories ("boys wearing hoodies are likely to be muggers," "people with regional accents are less well-educated," "men who went to Oxbridge are leadership material") are the stereotypes which are the basis of discrimination.

The power of implicit associations

These stereotypes, or implicit associations, seem to exist whatever our explicit beliefs and intentions, and that's because they're formed by our environment, in associative memory. It's an effortless way of learning, but it has drawbacks. If we repeatedly see women pushing vacuum cleaners, being helped to carry heavy objects, or giggling at assertive male behaviour, our memory stores the associations. If we continually see men holding sports trophies, or hear them expressing strong opinions in meetings, or interrupting female colleagues, we store those memories too.

You can explore your own implicit associations by taking the Harvard Implicit Association Test online (details in the *Exploring further* section at the end of this chapter). And one thing you will find is we are all biased in some way.

Why we hold onto stereotypes

The reason why it's so hard to overcome the stereotypes we've created is that we like to be right. Being right, or feeling assured that we've made the right judgement, *feels* good at a neurological level – it activates the brain's reward circuitry. We ignore our biases and are quick to justify our prejudices because to acknowledge them would feel actively unpleasant.

How does this actually work in the brain? Studies have shown that when people are doing a task that is boring and with no monetary reward, just doing the task correctly activates the areas of the brain linked to feelings of reward – the ventral striatum. And we get that pleasure of being right both when we *are* right and when we just *believe* we're right.

Being wrong (like being caught wrong-footed, or finding ourselves in the socially-unacceptable opinion group) feels bad. It activates the brain's "pain system" (the dorsal anterior cingulate and the anterior insula) which generate negative emotions such as anger and frustration and "social pain".

Feeling good when we're right, and pain when we're wrong means we're motivated to move on and not dig too deeply into decisions. None of us like to think of ourselves as biased. But just as most of us probably pictured a male head of technology in the journey-to-work anecdote, a study by Vanderbilt University's Cecilia Mo found implicit bias among both women and men. Using an Implicit Association Test she found even people who describe themselves as feminists still have a slight tendency – on average – to associate men with leadership.

Regardless of our sincerely-held beliefs, implicit biases can creep into our thinking and our decision-making, working against our own identities, and even our own careers.

Holding onto stereotypes despite our own experience

Once a stereotype has been adopted, it becomes a filter through which we selectively recall and use information. A study by Kevin

Dickson, at Southeast Missouri State University and Alicia Lorenz, found that people retain their stereotypical views, even when their personal experience presents evidence contradicting a stereotype. Even though we, the authors, are deeply involved in writing this book and both strongly believe in the power of women at work to do anything they set their minds to, both Jan and Francesca have found themselves at different times making assumptions based on stereotypes: women can't challenge a delay in their promotion, it's ok for men to dominate meetings, the CEOs going to be a man...

Girls do so well at school: why don't they rule the workplace?

The paradox of the stereotypes which hold women back in life is that their power flies in the face of girls' early development and exemplary school performance.

Biologically, girls are set up with a developmental advantage in key areas. They have longer attention spans, more advanced verbal and fine-motor skills, and greater social adeptness. They learn to speak before boys do, and read before boys do, and their emotional control functions mature years earlier. A study at Newcastle University by Marcus Kaiser found this can start for girls at 10 years of age whilst boys have to wait until 15 to 20 years old.

Typically, girls are better-behaved and more focused in class, they're eager to contribute and answer questions and they consistently score higher marks than boys of the same age. Stanford psychology professor Carol Dweck, who researches what she calls the mindset for success, says: "If life were one long grade school, women would be the undisputed rulers of the world."

Good behaviour doesn't rule the world

Many primary school teachers will tell you: girls are a pleasure to teach – they work hard and don't cause a lot of trouble. But here's the rub. School is where many girls are first rewarded for being good – instead of being energetic, rambunctious, adventurous or even pushy.

They learn that they are most in favour when they do things the right way: neatly and quietly. "They get a lot of praise for being perfect," says Dweck. In turn, they begin to seek the approval they get for being good, and this helps to establish a set of compliant behaviours, and a fixed mind-set (see Chapter 8 in the other half of this book).

But being a "good girl" doesn't prepare us very well for the real world.

The benefits of messing-about

Many girls learn to avoid taking risks and making mistakes. And psychologists now believe that risk-taking, failure and perseverance are essential confidence-building behaviours. Boys are told off and punished more, especially at school, and in the process, they learn to take failure in their stride. "When we observed in grade school classrooms, we saw that boys got eight times more criticism than girls for their conduct," Dweck writes. Complicating matters, she says, girls and boys get different patterns of feedback. "Boys' mistakes are attributed to a lack of effort while girls come to see mistakes as a reflection of their deeper qualities."

Boys also benefit from the lessons they learn – or teach one another – during playtime. From early on they are more physical, and more inclined to point out one another's limitations and call each other names. In the process, Dweck says, the criticisms and insults lose a lot of their power, making the boys more resilient.

Other psychologists have done work to show this playground mentality encourages men to be more resilient and to take negative feedback and criticism lightly. Similarly, on the sports field, boys learn not only to relish winning but also to deal with losing. These childhood experiences begin to build behaviour patterns and beliefs about how to be in the world.

Not all women are girly, not all men are blokes

In recognising the advantages of stereotypically male behaviour in the world of work, there's a tendency to conflate gender and assume that all men are blokey blokes and all women are feminine. But as Nikhil understands, the truth is that "feminine" traits can be part of a man's style and "masculine" traits can be part of a woman's.

How women are perceived has consequences for their performance evaluations, work relationships and promotion. If they match the stereotype they may be *liked* but not seen as competent, says psychologist Susan Fiske and her colleagues; if they demonstrate more masculine traits they may be judged as competent but not liked. (More on this research in chapter 11.) And other research has found men who display more feminine behaviours characteristics get judged as less competent in the same way that women do.

In the iconic ad-world TV series *Mad Men*, Joan used all her feminine wiles to exert influence whilst the boyish Peggy challenged stereotypes and fought for promotion.

In their study of the workplace, mother-and-daughter researchers Joan Williams and Rachel Dempsey found that 73% of women interviewed reported problems finding a balance between being seen as too feminine or too masculine. And though the media would have us believe that it's hard-ass women who succeed in business, nearly twice as many successful business women (66%) reported having problems related to being too feminine, such as being described as too soft, too collaborative and not assertive enough, compared with 34% being seen as too masculine.

Playing to the stereotype

But do we have a choice about whether we adhere to stereotypes or not? The work of Judith Butler at University of California, Berkeley, suggests masculine and feminine behaviour is all a "performance" based on socialisation and society's expectations, and that we don't have to act in this prescribed manner. "When we say gender is performed," Butler explains, "we usually mean that we've taken on a role or we're acting in some way and that our acting or our role playing is crucial to the gender that we are and the gender that we present to the world."

Evidence of this "performance" also comes from studies by Stacy Sinclair from Princeton University who has found that people "tune in" to a situation and comply with what they believe are the expectations of the others involved. Self-conceptions adjust to create a shared reality. So, when the expectations of us are stereotypical, our behaviour follows suit.

For example, one group of women were told they were going to meet with a charming, sexist man, who thought women should be cared for and protected. They subsequently rated themselves as more stereotypically feminine, and were judged to behave in more stereotypical ways when they met the man (an actor), compared with another group of women who were expecting to interact with a man with more contemporary views.

This social tuning only seems to happen when there is motivation for a good relationship. So, just as Nikhil felt he had to adjust his behaviour to fit with his more macho male colleagues, will Siobhan be more susceptible to "fluttering her eyelashes" at work when she needs to impress?

An end to stereotypes?

In the Head Heart + Brain survey there was evidence that these expectations were breaking down. Women believed they must be recognised for their abilities and achievements, but also that they had to succeed without upsetting the hierarchy and senior male expectations – or at least not upsetting them too much.

Subverting the stereotypes

Some women believed that playing a stereotypical feminine role helped to build relationships and collaboration and was good for team work. It was also felt to be helpful at the start of a career when they needed to build a reputation for competence and co-operation. One woman acknowledged that she worked the stereotype of women being better at relationships to get herself on a high-profile project that was having issues forming a collaborative working team.

But they were also aware they would have to be prepared to stand their corner when necessary. One participant said holding back until you were sure of your understanding, and then asking the killer question, could be a good method of disarming people and building a reputation for being highly competent, especially in a technical role.

Many of the respondents were quite willing to turn the stereotypes to their own advantage when they saw an opportunity. Not quite "playing the dumb blonde," but one woman told us she allowed her prejudiced male colleagues to assume she was no good at maths because to have demonstrated her ability would have been threatening to them.

We may have our own views of whether it's acceptable to use a stereotypical assumption to your advantage; these participants felt it went some way to redressing the balance of stereotypes that worked against them.

What kind of training will be effective?

Acknowledging stereotypes are prevalent, mitigating their impact and recognising that things will only change permanently when the associations between roles and gender change, are what will make the difference at work.

Many organisations have introduced checks and balances to minimise the impact of bias, such as recruitment systems which present blind shortlists with no gender details and which highlight biased job descriptions and requirements. And 20% of major US companies now provide training to address unconscious bias.

But gender bias is not solved by increasing people's knowledge. Gender bias, as with any other bias, largely happens at an unconscious level, and training individuals can raise awareness, but will not overcome it.

Deep change

People need to interrupt their System 1 quick decisions and their implicit associations, and that only comes with either deep personal change or a systematic approach in the organisation to design policy and decision-making practices that nudge people to take the right action, or bypass the bias. Work on eliminating gender bias is just beginning to happen in this area, largely inspired by Harvard behavioural economist Iris Bohnet's findings on how to use brain functions to mitigate our biases.

But combating bias could be deceptively simple. The single most effective way to bring about change is for us all to slow down and give ourselves time to reflect on decisions before they're implemented. Recent research by social neuroscientists Jay Van Bavel and Daniel Yudkin at New York University found that when participants had "high cognitive load" - they were making decisions quickly or had to be thinking about several things at once (as we so frequently have to do at work) – they were biased towards their own group. When participants had time to slow down and reflect, there was no evidence of bias.

When people are able to notice and overcome bias, it's been observed that the regions associated with inhibition – the ventrolateral prefrontal cortex (VLPFC) – which neuroscientist Matt Lieberman has termed the brain's "braking system" is activated. When people are able to apply their mental brake they take a more objective view and check their assumptions, and unconscious bias can be mitigated.

As one of the participants in the Head Heart + Brain survey commented, what's necessary for success is to give the issue of gender bias "the space, air-time and budget it deserves, recognising that an organisation that works to achieve gender equality will be high-performing."

Career hacks

Develop self-awareness

We believe that being self-aware is essential to working more effectively, whether you're a man or a woman. Being mindful of what is going on day-to-day at work is one way of increasing self-awareness. (You can read more about self-awareness and how to develop it in Chapter 9 of the other half of this book). And slowing down and noticing your own thinking is one way to be more aware.

Notice more

As you go through a day, be alert to subtle signals that indicate "it's a man's world" or "it's a woman's world". For example, men being praised for their ideas, being asked to an important client meeting when they are not on the account, or socialising with more senior people.

Signals that it's a women's world might be a powerful group of women who set the tone in the business, women being asked their opinion more frequently than men, or women having easy access to senior leaders. Once you've identified the behaviours, you can decide which ones you want to mirror.

Identify your own style

The Bem sex roles inventory (named after Cornell psychologist the late Sandra Bem) is the standard test used for assessing gender roles. Over a couple of days keep this check-list of traits adapted from the inventory at hand, and make a note whenever you see a personal trait that matches the stereotype. Notice how you behave in meetings, with those who are more junior or more senior to you, when you are relaxed and what's different when you are stressed or under pressure, and how you act with people you're comfortable with compared with those you don't know very well.

Demonstrating masculine traits	Matches	Demonstrating feminine traits	Matches
Assertiveness		Being affectionate	
Ambition		Cheerfulness	
Showing Competitiveness		Compassion	
Forcefulness		Gentleness	
Leadership capability		Openness	
Independence		Shyness	
Individualism		Speaking softly	
Decisiveness		Sympathy	
Tough-mindedness		Kindness	
Self-sufficiency		Tenderness	
Risk-taking		Understanding	

You can then use this awareness to either play up or play down the character trait in different circumstances: you might decide to be less tough-minded with a junior, or more tender with someone who is experiencing personal problems, or make decisions more decisively.

Exercise positivity

If you are working in an organisation where stereotypes create bias and – like Siobhan – you're finding this challenging – you may be finding that giving the best of yourself day after day in an organisation that is biased is deeply demoralising. You need to balance this with some positivity.

We all know it's easier to manage challenging situations when we're in a positive frame of mind, and extensive work over many years by psychologist Barbara Fredrickson at North Carolina has found the many beneficial effects of positive emotions. In the context of problem-solving and decision-making, a positive mood and good team environment have been shown to create more insight, produce more creativity and mould a team that performs to a higher standard.

Fredrickson says that it's important to achieve a ratio of 3:1 positive experiences to negative experiences. This appears to be the optimum. People and teams then are more open to new ideas as the brain goes into approach or reward mode, which results in people picking up more contextual information, making more connections and being better able to read other people's emotions.

Regularly recording your personal positivity helps to give you a sense of progress and avoid the distortion that comes with remembering only bad experiences. (Details of Fredrickson's Positivity Test are in *Exploring further* at the end of this chapter.)

Develop some Smooth Comebacks

You will need to have some effective and acceptable responses ready to deploy when you encounter sexism and put-downs.

It's useful to practise them so you get the tone and timing right (saying something immediately can be effective with a peer who makes a sexist comment, but you might want to have the conversation in private when it's your boss).

If co-workers are making sexist comments, come back with: "Think about what you just said. Do you really believe that's OK?" Or, "Joking aside guys, how would you feel if that was said about your girlfriend, or your sister?"

If your boss continually asks you to get the coffee, you might want to say with a smile, "It's Mike's turn." Better still, agree with your peers there will be a rota, and have the next person who is due to get the coffee volunteer: "It's my turn."

And if its someone very senior like the CEO you might want to make the comment privately or with a lighter note. Try something like: "I know you really care about the culture here and I just want to say I don't think that comment/joke really gives the right impression of who we are as a company."

By mentally rehearsing your responses you start to build the neural networks for a new behaviour. (The brain can't tell the difference between imagining something and doing it.) Practise your phrase, your tone of voice *and* how you will hold yourself, so that when the response is required it will come confidently.

Invest in understanding yourself

Our *personal* recommendation for a response to sexism is to be bold, be yourself and act from what you believe.

When someone is self-aware and purposeful in what they are doing, they are less likely to generate an aggressive reaction. Authentic behaviour resonates even when it runs counter to the norm. So, invest in understanding yourself and what's important to you, where to draw a line, which challenges to fight and which to let go.

Learn to understand your own behaviour, the micro-gestures and tone you use automatically, good and bad, and how you manage your emotions. (Many of us have taken years to understand this: start early and reap the benefits!)

A very practical approach, which is highly effective, is sharing what you know about yourself. This might sound ridiculously self-absorbed, but it's disarmingly successful. While it's often considered unacceptable to appear ambitious, consider how it sounds if a colleague says: "I enjoy giving presentations," "I want to learn more about negotiating," or "I'm ready for more responsibility." Or even "I'm ambitious". Negativity comes from other people applying a label to you – rarely from being honest and transparent.

Siobhan and Nikhil now know how stereotypes are created and how bias affects both men and women. They're determined to avoid letting it define their own careers and to stand up to it at work whenever they can.

Siobhan is working out some Smooth Comebacks with some women friends, and is also teaming up with a male colleague to see if they can change some of their boss's sexist behaviour. She's practising saying "I really enjoy a challenge"!

Nikhil is working on recognising his own work style. And he has managed to say "Nah, that's not the kind of thing I enjoy," when invited to join some of the laddish behaviour.

Exploring further

Books

Thinking Fast and Slow, Daniel Kahneman

What Works: Gender Equality By Design, Iris Bohnet

What Works for Women at Work – Four Patterns Women Need to Know, Joan Williams and Rachel Dempsey

Mindset: The New Psychology of Success, Carol Dweck

Articles, blogs and podcasts

When Talking About Bias Backfires, Adam Grant and Sheryl Sandberg (Revealing insights into how knowledge about the prevalence of stereotypes can actually lead to more stereotyping.) New York Times

Inclusive Leadership, Stereotyping and the Brain (After decades of efforts within corporations to reduce prejudice and encourage diversity, why is it still so hard to keep discrimination out of the workplace?) Keynote address, panel discussion and pdf of Columbia Business School's research symposium.

Videos and webinars

Creating a Level Playing Field, Shelley Correll (How errors in judgment and evaluation contribute to a gap in opportunities for women.) Stanford University (28:34)

What works for Women at Work, Joan Williams (Four gender biases and how to navigate them at work.) Stanford University (11:35)

What happens when we "un-box" each other (An advertisement for a Danish TV station that graphically illustrates "categorisation" has gone viral.) YouTube (3:00)

Inspiring the Future – Redraw The Balance (Primary school children reveal the reality of gender stereotyping when asked to draw firefighters, surgeons, fighter pilots: 61 drawn as men, 5 as women. And then they met the real women in those jobs. [NB the Comments posted by viewers express a pungent range of biased opinion.]) YouTube (2:07)

Feminism for 5 year olds (In a trailer for Channel 4's series The Secret Life of 5 Year Olds, Eva shakes up the stereotypes.) facebook.com/Channel4

The science of inclusion, Quinetta Roberson (How to enhance fairness in work teams, and how the management of diversity can improve organisational effectiveness.) TEDx (10:10)

50/50, Tiffany Shlain (Where are we on the 10,000-year arc of women and power? And what's it going to take to get to a #5050 world and a better gender balance for everyone?) YouTube (20:28)

The surprising neuroscience of gender inequality, Janet Crawford (An empowering talk challenging both men and women to shift the balance from blame to action, through engagement and curiosity.) TEDx (12:38)

Thinking, Fast and Slow, Daniel Kahneman (The Nobel prize-winning psychologist whose work has challenged the rational model of judgment and decision-making in economics, medicine, and politics, has never brought his many years of research and thinking together in one book.) Talks at Google (01:02:06)

Ballroom dance that breaks gender roles, Trevor Copp and Jeff Fox (Tango, waltz, foxtrot... the man always leads and the woman always follows. That's an idea worth changing: two ballroom dance instructors demonstrate their "Liquid Lead" dance technique.) TEDx (15:34)

And also...

Implicit Association Test, Project Implicit (Test your own implicit associations by taking the online test. NB its application has been challenged by some scientists because the results are not reliably replicable, by the same person from one day to the next.) Harvard University

The Positivity Self-Test, Barbara Fredrickson (Fredrickson believes that experiencing positive emotions in a 3-to-1 ratio to negative emotions leads to numerous benefits. Take the online test to measure your own positivity ratio.) positivityratio.com

3.
Understanding the minefield of office dress code

Towards the end of her first year at Multinational Trading Siobhan is still trying to figure out what's appropriate to wear for work, and how that fits with her personal style, and her budget. At her graduate scheme review her HR manager suggested she might consider investing a little more in her working wardrobe, and go for a more corporate look. Siobhan isn't really sure what that means. Can they even say that?

What to wear to work can be a minefield for women and we debated between ourselves about whether we should include it in this book. After all it's not really anything to do with our brains. Or is it?

Before we embark on working life we're used to dressing to suit ourselves, to express our personalities. We might be playing with different looks, or just dressing purely for practicality and not caring about what our clothes say about our gender, intelligence or femininity. Or that's what many of us like to believe.

De-coding the code

Now all of a sudden at work there is a dress code to follow – and it is a code. Scientific studies have shown that we register the smallest details of appearance within the first moments of meeting someone: within around 30milliseconds we have made a judgement. Clothes are symbols of masculinity and femininity and are linked to stereotypes and associations of how competent you are, how intelligent and how trustworthy.

Back in the late 1990s Jeff Hearn and David Collinson from Manchester and Warwick universities were writing on the essential masculinity of management structures and that when people think of a manager they think of (see) a male body. This adds to the hurdles women have to fit in. In addition, they observed that the advice guides on appropriate office attire recommended a style of masculine fashion for working women: dark suits, neutral shirts, no pink or frills, and definitely not too much skin or cleavage to announce your femininity. Is that good advice for Siobhan?

Just following the rules

Following the rules may feel safe. The need to conform is a widespread feature of animal behaviour, observed in species from monkeys following the leader's cues of when to eat, travel and socialise, to humpback whales following the pod. Scientists believe that learning to conform maintained our all-important membership of the social group which supported us in finding shelter and food, and a mate (much like the modern workplace, then!).

In this day and age, we like to think that clothing is a trivial, and trivialising, subject – not one we should waste much time on. It feels wrong if we find ourselves commenting on what an authoritative woman speaker is wearing: Teresa May's kitten heels, Angela Merkel's boxy suits, Nicola Sturgeons' stilettos, Christine Lagarde's elegance... It seems their clothes shouldn't be worthy of our attention: we wouldn't objectify a man in the same way.

Except that... we do notice what men wear, and men themselves are acutely aware of the fine distinctions in their own more constrained dress codes. One of our survey participants, a young man starting his career in the education sector said "I feel that the attire expected of a male working in an office has not always moved with the times. Thankfully, my female colleagues are not expected to wear high heels, makeup or impeccable dresses (unless this is a personal choice), so many wear casual attire to the office unless they see a client or other stakeholder. Yet this informal ruling doesn't seem to apply to the male section of the workforce. Men are not expected to wear suits but should still wear appropriate suit trousers or chinos and shirt. It's commented on if anyone strays from this path."

Fitness: the new appearance test

Non-conformist office dressers can face strong social sanctions. For men, the codes used to be polished shoes and the brand of watch. Now it's the cut of their jackets, the length of their trousers, even the colour of the shirt and of course the minefield of tie or no-tie. And now a newly rigorous standard of body shape and fitness is added to the coded requirements for both men and women.

A 2017 study by Stockholm University's Janet Johansson has found that a healthy, fit and athletic body is a key marker in how male managers, are judged. Managers who are physically fit and toned, and who dress in a disciplined manner, are judged as more effective than managers who are overweight or untidy. Johansson said, "The top managers outline a role-script that is mainly characterized with self-disciplinary qualities and masculine values, they define the leadership context with athleticism in the centre, and they express an overt intent to elevate some people and exclude others in organizational processes based on athletic values in which they personally believe."

Dressing sexy

This is a specifically athletic definition of "fit." Sexy is not a power-dressing style. A 2005 study by psychologist Peter Glick at Lawrence University confirmed what we might believe: that women managers who dressed "sexily" were rated more harshly than a receptionist who dressed in the same way. "Sexy self-presentation harms women in high-, but not low-status jobs," the authors concluded.

"It's really difficult to navigate the dress/appearance norms as a woman in business" commented a 55 year-old female HR executive in the UK in our survey. "Trying to come across as both feminine and serious, and express your individuality... it's a minefield!"

And as for the vexed issue of high heels for women at work, a 2017 study by Maxwell Barnish at the University of Aberdeen found that both men and women find heels more "attractive" due to what are described as "complex cultural reasons." They also found that high heels influence male managers' behaviour: they are more likely to help a woman in high heels and to do favours for them.

So there is the dilemma: you may want to wear high heels because they give you confidence, put you on eye-level with male colleagues, or you just think they "look better." But you need to decide whether you want to benefit from the kind of stereotypically-triggered assistance that they may encourage.

The vertiginously high heels worn by Facebook COO Sheryl Sandberg at a World Economic Forum have been considered photo newsworthy. But teamed with tailored mono-coloured jackets and shift dresses the look is designed to signal power and competence rather than sex appeal. And it's worth noting that Sandberg expertly adapts her dress style to her context, wearing notably more relaxed clothing and flat shoes, signalling "warmth", when she's with her perpetually t-shirted boss Mark Zuckerberg.

Quit or fit

Unless your workplace dress code is outright sexist or demeaning (and a requirement to wear high heels as a receptionist, or a frilled apron and cap as a hotel room maid might meet your definition of sexist) you either need to fit in or quit.

How well you "fit" with the office dress code is a lot to do with how well you feel you personally fit with the organisation – or your perception of it, at this stage of your career. Can you be yourself, are they your kind of people, does it reflect your values? Do you *want* to fit in, and you just don't understand the dress rules (or you haven't figured out how to dress corporately on your salary?)

Or is some of your unease about the idea of appropriate workwear a reflection of ambivalence about the organisation? We know from neuroscience research by Jay Van Bavel at New York University that when people want to be part of a group (in this case, the organisation you work for), they are highly motivated to conform to the norms of that group and will even change their own beliefs to fit with the group. (See Chapter 10 in the other half of this book)

How to react to feedback

Barbed comments about dress that are just sexist or belittling need a Smooth Comeback (see Chapter 2 in this half of the book) to quickly highlight their inappropriateness. But more formal advice about work clothing that links it to our job prospects needs to be considered differently.

Being advised on what to wear and how to dress is something many women have to contend with. And the substance of the "advice" is often shockingly inappropriate. A 2016 study by legal firm Slater and Gordon of 2,000 UK working women found that almost one in ten women have been told by their boss to wear more make-up, high heels, more revealing tops or shorter skirts at work. And these weren't women in "display roles": they included IT, legal, banking, HR and healthcare employees. A depressing 86% of those who suffered this form of discrimination felt their career might suffer if they didn't acquiesce to their boss's direction (despite it being illegal in the UK to make such a request).

Equally, one respondent to the Head Heart + Brain survey, a 30 year-old female retail manager working in eastern Europe, reported: "I was told at interview that I needed to balance my femininity, and that I should wear a trouser suit."

There are of course degrees of feedback on dress, some of it clearly illegal and some trying to be helpful. We can quickly feel trivialised if someone at work gives us direction about what we should wear ("Never mind that – you hired me for my brains...."). This may be where we would be wise to pause and consider our response to any feedback which may be triggering an "amygdala hijack" in the brain: that feeling where you experience so much threat that you are lost for words. And after consideration, it's likely you will feel a long-term threat to your CORE elements, especially your sense of reputation and options (see Brain Basics in Chapter 1 in the other half of the book).

Assessing the quality of feedback

Feedback feels like criticism – and it hurts. And criticism of our clothing feels especially personal. The old adage of "don't take the advice of anyone you don't respect" may come into play. You need to evaluate the standpoint and intentions of the person giving you the feedback.

If it's a notoriously conservative manager commenting on your office-wear you might feel free to ignore his views – while being aware that you could be endangering your chances for promotion in that direction. If the feedback is coming from an HR manager you might evaluate it differently. By and large, no-one raises the subjects of clothing, or personal hygiene, lightly: HR professionals will tell you that these discussions always feel awkwardly personal.

This might be the moment for a reflective step-back: is it possible that this feedback is well-intentioned advice about something that is relatively easy for you to change, which will otherwise affect your career progression?

Understand the rules before you change them

The participants in the Head Heart + Brain research agreed that women need to be sensitive to workplace norms: dress codes will be different in a bank or a law firm to a design agency. Within those norms, you can choose what works for you and suits your personality, but don't lose sight of the impression it creates for other people.

"I've had it both ways," said a 56 year-old communications executive in the UK: "Looking too mainstream wearing Marks & Spencer in a creative organisation; and having my (woman) boss in a charity comment 'You always wear such amazing clothes' – which seemed to suggest I wasn't quite serious enough to fit in."

If you want to change the rules and, for example, run the first real estate firm where your agents wear jeans rather than suits, first of all you have to work your way up to being the boss. Women leaders in the funeral industry, for example, have signalled their new approach to managing death by wearing bright colours.

Not conforming

There is research that shows, once you have proven your competence, having some distinctive or quirky aspect to your dress can be advantage.

A series of studies by researchers at Columbia and Harvard business schools have found that breaking the rules can sometimes boost your social standing. Luxury store salespeople attributed higher status and wealth to casually-dressed shoppers. And executives saw unconventionally dressed staffers as more competent. Researchers call this the "red sneaker effect," and we all know someone like the ace computer technician who can turn up to work wearing a t-shirt and low-slung jeans because he's essential to the smooth running of the organisation's IT system.

The studies demonstrate that people ascribe higher status and competence, and a perceived autonomy, to people who don't completely conform to the norms. But it's a delicate balance to achieve. The judgements depended on the value placed on uniqueness in the person making the judgement - that's usually your boss or your client. And the positive judgements can disappear when the observer is in an unfamiliar environment, or when the nonconforming behaviour is seen as unintentional (you're just "not quite getting it right" rather than deliberately expressing your personality).

Siobhan will be wise to curtail her quirky dress-sense at work if her boss just doesn't "get it,", and avoid wearing the red sneakers the first time a new client comes to the office.

The power to be different

Columbia's Silvia Bellezza explains that social capital is like currency, and those who intentionally break the rules appear to be able to afford it. So, for example, at the start of the Trump presidency, when it appeared that the president had a strong preference for "women dressing like women" in the White House, and smart corporate suits for men, it was his then chief strategist Steve Bannon's no-tie, khaki-pants, unshaven look which spoke volumes about his position of power.

Likewise, Rebekah Brooks, CEO of News UK (previously News International) was known for her dramatic free-flowing curly red hair. Rupert Murdoch's right-hand-woman in the UK did not need a conventionally corporate haircut.

Other research suggests leaders who have a distinctive style are the people we value the most and are inspired to imitate. A newly-hired, highly respected woman who wears smart suits with beautifully draped scarves can quickly inspire other women in an organisation to adopt the same style. At the bank where author Jan worked the new CEO had a habit of throwing the ends of his tie over his shoulder at lunch: Jan surmised he'd had soup spillage issues at some point, but was amused to see that within weeks all the senior males were doing the same.

What clothes say about our status and competence

We know, of course, that what we wear is an outward signal of status. Psychologist Peter Glick confirms that how a woman (or a man) dresses sends a message about her social status: should she be deferred too, looked up to or dismissed? And our brains keep a very careful check on our social ranking: is our reputation better than the others in the group, or worse?

Critically, research has also found that conforming to dress codes impacts on perceptions of our personality and our abilities. Women who dress in a masculine fashion during a job interview are more likely to be hired, and a teaching assistant who wears formal clothes is perceived as more intelligent than one who dresses more casually.

Glick wrote in 2016 that how women dress determines whether they are perceived as "warm" or "competent" (more on that in Chapter 11 in this half of the book). If a woman dresses too attractively (she's too "warm"), she risks not being taken as seriously as a more "competent" woman who dresses more severely. And although Glick considers only the judgements made by men, other research has found women – finely attuned to reading these social nuances – are often the harshest judges of another woman's appearance.

Our research showed that many women clearly understand these judgements and make decisions every day to restrain expressing their personality through what they wear in order to conform to accepted stereotypes. One of our research participants said she loves fashion but at work always wears a "uniform" of dark suit, light shirt and scarf. Her belief is that there would otherwise be judgement of her attire, and of her personality.

Clothes and mood

Do you wear clothing that reflects your mood, or do you wear clothing to change your mood? Researchers from the University of Queensland interviewed people and observed their clothing choices to find out.

The answer was that, more often than not, we dress according to how we'd *like* to feel, or how we'd like others to think we're feeling. And it works, especially if you wear clothes that have won compliments in the past, inspire confidence or bring back positive memories. This is the concept of "enclothed cognition": the influence clothes have on the wearer's thoughts and feelings (that is, what our clothes say *to* us, not about us: how they make us feel).

Dressing to change our mood

University of Hertfordshire psychologist Karen Pine has tested the link between mood and clothing and found that "happy" clothes – the ones that make us feel good – are well-cut, figure-enhancing, and made from bright, quality fabrics. "Clothing doesn't just influence others," says Pine, "it reflects and influences the wearer's mood too. Many of the women in this study felt they could alter their mood by changing what they wore. This demonstrates the psychological power of clothing and how the right choices could influence a person's happiness."

Clothes also affect our perception of our abilities: Pine gave her students superhero t-shirts to wear and found that those dressed as superheroes thought they were more likeable, *and* rated themselves as physically stronger that students in plain t-shirts. The same results are found with more conventional work-wear: researchers have found that test subjects given a number of challenging cognitive tests felt significantly more powerful and in control of the situation when dressed in formal business attire compared with their casually-dressed peers.

Clothes *affect* our competence

But not only that – they *were actually* more competent: they could think faster on their feet and had more creative ideas.

Adam Galinsky of Northwestern University examined the remarkable effects of enclothed cognition in a 2012 study which showed that if you put on a white coat that you believe belongs to a doctor, your ability to pay attention increases sharply. If you're told that it's a house-painter's coat, you'll show no improvement in ability. And a decade earlier psychologist Barbara Fredrickson found that women scored lower in a maths test when they were wearing a swimsuit. (Though men's scores were unaffected by what they wore.)

Fredrickson suggested that self-objectification consumes mental resources, but men are less concerned by it and so are able to keep focused on the task. All of which suggests that we need to dress not to express how we feel, but how we *want* to feel. We need to find a style of clothing for work that is the acceptable equivalent of the superhero t-shirt: actively boosting confidence, and competence, without becoming a distraction.

Find a style and stick to it

Clothes, whether we like it or not, are part of our personal brand: "This is me." And having a consistent image is reassuring for the people we work with. But is it enough to establish an acceptable style of dress for work at the start of your career, as Siobhan is attempting to do?

Is the wardrobe you established when you first started work sending the message you want to convey now that you're leading a team? As you progress you have an opportunity to communicate with your clothes: "This is the advanced me."

Making changes at career transitions is a powerful way of signalling your ambitions. The brain is a pattern recognition machine: it likes to be able to predict ("I'll take Siobhan to the client meeting – she'll look appropriate."). When you subtly change your style you communicate your readiness for promotion, or let people know that they now need to relate to you differently.

And just as the brain desires certainty, it also responds to novelty; this is your opportunity to ratchet up your style, and possibly add a little more personal flair that will make you memorable. Jay Van Bavel's research on out-groups and in-groups has found that once our membership of the in-group is firmly established we have more leeway to express our individuality.

In the meantime, follow the lead of someone that you respect, and acknowledge the dress norms. And if you want to dress distinctively remember you are sending a significant signal and be prepared to live with it. With individualised style, as with quality dressing, we could do worse than follow the advice of Coco Chanel: "Dress shabbily; people remember the clothes. Dress impeccably; people remember the woman."

Career hacks

Dress for success

Whilst we don't want to tell you how to dress a few simple principles may help.

Dress for effectiveness

• Get started with a store that has personal shopping service, or take along a "critical friend" who has a good eye.
• Choose clothes that fit you perfectly and feel physically good. Learn what kind of style and shape flatters you, and which colours suit your personality and skin tone.
• If you're aiming to step up your appearance to the next level to signal ambition and competence it should be an extension of your current style rather than a radical new look.
• Once you make the shift, stick with it.

Smart shopping

• Avoid buying pieces you love that don't "go with" anything you own: these will be the items that hang unworn in your wardrobe.
• Focus on outfit shopping so that you have a complete look to wear straight away. And take the first opportunity to wear it, to incorporate it into your "look".
• In the sales, each season buy one work outfit which is above your normal price range. A well-chosen, expensive piece will boost your confidence and status.
• Create a small collection of the best-quality accessories you can afford and never give them away unless they have a very strong negative association. The scarf you tire of may be the statement piece you want years later.
• Plan to cull your wardrobe twice a year: hang all your hangers the wrong way round at the beginning of the season, and only turn them the right way when you wear the item. Anything still facing the wrong way at the end of the season should go.
• Donate clothes that no longer fit – let someone else enjoy them.

Dress to improve your mood

- Consider both how you want to feel and the impression you want to create.
- Notice how outfits make you feel: calm, confident, powerful, playful... then choose what you wear according to the mood you want that day.
- Resist buying clothes that are "out of your comfort zone": you won't feel like yourself and you'll find you don't wear them or you have a 'bad day" when you do.
- Cull clothes which have negative associations: they're just taking up wardrobe space.

Dress for ease / practicality

- Choose fabrics that are easy to wear, don't crease too much and flatter your body shape.
- Avoid clothes which you have to constantly adjust: the top which gapes or the skirt which rides up. Anything that needs tweaking in the changing room will be unhelpful in daily wear.
- Rotate what you wear. It's easy to fall into the habit of putting on the same items: "It's Tuesday, I'll wear the blue dress."

Siobhan is willing to take clothes more seriously after considering the strength of the research. She has decided to enlist the help of a girlfriend whose judgement she trusts, who has a slightly more senior corporate role, to help her find her office style. She's bearing in mind No Red Sneakers until she's senior enough to pull off a really out-there look.

Exploring further

Books

You Are What You Wear: What Your Clothes Reveal About You,
Jennifer Baumgartner

Mind What You Wear, Karen Pine

Articles, blogs and podcasts

Why Workplace Dress Codes Have Troubled Women for Decades,
Emma Bell (Organisational behaviourist Bell argues that wearing
high heels at work is a game women cannot win.) Newsweek.com

Confidence Dressing: How Clothing Affects the Mind, Katherine
Bernard (Discussion of research in which subjects who wore white
coats they thought belonged to doctors performed better on tests.)
Vogue.com

Videos

Why dressing for success works, Wall Street Journal (How suiting-up
can give you a leg up at work.) wsj.com (4:02)

The Way We Dress: The Transformative Power of Clothes (Our
sartorial choices manifest as an extension of ourselves: a reflection
of our personalities.) Nowness.com (2:57)

4.
What they say, and the way that they say it

It's 18 months into Siobhan and Nikhil's careers at Multinational Trading Ltd, and Siobhan is feeling she's not fitting into the organisation in the same way as Nikhil. As a female she's always outnumbered in meetings and the guys in her team all have a lot to say. She reckons she knows as much as they do, and more in some areas, but she just can't get her voice heard.

There are more women in Nikhil's team and one of them is regarded as "a bit of a ball-breaker". She seems to be quite opinionated, and a couple of times she's called out guys for interrupting. She may get her voice heard, Nikhil tells Siobhan, but she isn't winning the popularity vote.

A 54-year-old woman who works in a government department in the UK told the Head Heart + Brain survey: "[In my organisation] the attributes of successful people are often described in terms which could be seen as male: 'thrusting', 'analytical', 'relentless', 'self-confident', 'determined;' rather than 'collegiate,' 'team builder,' 'engaging,' 'supportive.'"

Another research participant commented that the latest management fads often adopt a masculine terminology. For example, the Agile software delivery method is all about "Scrum Masters."

These are the problems of gendered language and male-dominated dialogue that women contend with every day at work. Do they matter?

The power of words

When we say "he" when referring to a prospective IT specialist we are both perpetuating a stereotype and alienating women in those roles from feeling they belong.

Studies by social psychologists Jane Stout and Nilanjana Dasgupta have demonstrated the power of language to define and exclude us at work. They found that both men and women identified gender-exclusive language as sexist, but women nevertheless responded with a decreased sense of belonging, lower motivation, and identified less with their jobs compared with those who experienced gender-inclusive or gender-neutral language.

A study by cognitive scientist Lera Boroditsky suggests the gender associated with a word forms our understanding and the qualities we link to it. For example, the word "key" is masculine in German and feminine in Spanish. Asked to describe a key, German speakers list hard attributes (hard, heavy, metal...) while Spanish speakers choose softer attributes (beautiful, elegant, fragile...).

And we know that language and cognition are deeply linked both consciously and unconsciously. A study by Ruud Custer at University College London has shown that holding a hot cup of coffee makes us feel more warmly towards the person we're talking to, and sitting on a hard chair makes us negotiate harder.

Taking action on language

As part of its anti-bias programme, UK telecom provider Vodafone discourages the use of gendered words such as "aggressive" when drafting its job advertisements ("Vodafone is pursuing an aggressive market-building strategy..."), which can discourage women applicants. Instead it substitutes neutral terms such as "bold." And there are a whole host of recruitment apps which screen for masculine language in an attempt to attract more women into jobs which have historically recruited men.

But a woman working in the construction industry in the UK, told Head Heart + Brain: "[The language] is not something that can realistically be challenged where I work. It's endemic – it's in the DNA of the business. If I attempt to raise it, with examples (as I have done in the past) it's seen as a bit of a joke. It's just not taken seriously or addressed."

We were disappointed to find very few companies taking action on this issue in our research, other than in recruitment advertising. Sexist language continues in talent, promotion and competency frameworks. And our research suggests derogatory language directed at women is still widespread, with nearly 40% of women saying they had experienced it, compared with less than 10% of men. And 45% of women also experienced belittling jokes, compared with 20% of men. One woman told us: "([I was] bullied after refusing to let a more senior person make inappropriate sexual remarks."

The new language of sexism

At the same time as we are becoming more aware of the effect of everyday language on women's expectations and performance, there are new words being coined to highlight sexist patterns of behaviour in conversations:

> *Manterrupting*: unnecessary interruption of a woman by a man
> *Mansplaining*: a man explaining to a woman in a condescending, overconfident manner, often completely unnecessarily
> *Manstanding*: talking excessively, or talking over a woman
> *Bropropriating*: a man taking credit for a woman's idea

To these we might add one of our own, *Manseeing*: when men only see and address their remarks to another man – regardless of the status of a woman who's present.

You know how it goes: the waiter who addresses his questions to the man at the table. The male speaker who only makes eye contact with the men sitting round the conference table. Or the house vendor handing over the keys to a million-pound home who explains how to read the meter to a young male colleague of the purchaser who's just carrying in some boxes, while the woman purchaser – whose name is actually on the contract – is standing alongside tapping her foot. (Is this sounding a little personal? Yes, it happened to me, and it rankled! Jan Hills).

The Head Heart + Brain research participants certainly recognised the behaviour that these new words label: they would be speaking in a meeting, only to be interrupted by a man. They might propose an idea, only to have a man make the same proposal five minutes later (as though it was new). Women told us they may have the creativity but men have the right vocal chords. Women don't get credit for their proposals, and as a result they tend to speak up less and lose their confidence.

A rich history of gendered language

The issues of speaking and language at work have attracted the attention of influential advocates. Facebook COO Sheryl Sandberg and Wharton business school professor Adam Grant wrote in one of a series of articles for the *New York Times* about the perils of "speaking while female": "We've both seen it happen again and again. When a woman speaks in a professional setting, she walks a tightrope. Either she's barely heard or she's judged as too aggressive. When a man says virtually the same thing, heads nod in appreciation for his fine idea."

Sandberg and Grant refer to a long line of research showing that when it comes to the workplace, women speak less, are interrupted more, and have their ideas more harshly scrutinised.

Specialists in gender language studies describe three models of conversation: Deficit, Difference and Dominance.

Deficit is usually attributed to the work of linguist Robin Lakoff who says women's language lacks confidence, because we have been socialised into speaking habits such as using "tag questions" at the end of sentences ("It's cold in here, isn't it?), "umms and aahs" and indirect requests ("It would be good if we could get the minutes circulated earlier") which all combine to signal lower social status.

Difference theory proposes that women's language is more centred on supporting the speaker, more cooperative especially in same-sex conversations and more concerned with being polite. (Men, by contrast, signal solidarity by using insults rather than positive politeness strategies.)

Dominance (reflecting men's social status) focuses on how men control conversations: interrupting more and being more vocal than women in mixed-sex conversation.

Many of these studies of language and gender date back to the 1970s through to the 1990s, and all of them embody some useful insights. But they also focus on difference rather than similarities, and to the extent that they define women's speaking style as the problem-that-needs-fixing, they do bolster a stereotype of under-confident women who don't help their own cause.

Speaking patterns at work today

Do the same behaviours still dominate the conversations that take place in workplaces today? A 2011 study quoted by Grant and Sandberg found that senior male US Senators speak significantly more than their junior colleagues, while female senior Senators do not. And male executives who speak more often than their peers are deemed to be 10% *more* competent, while female executives who speak up are considered *less* competent.

And also useful is the research which looks at the content and purpose of men's and women's different speaking styles. Deborah Tannen, influential professor of linguistics at Washington's Georgetown University, has explored men's and women's speech patterns and says that men tend to adopt a "report" talk pattern, and women a "rapport" talk pattern. Men speak to determine and achieve power and status. Women talk to determine and achieve connection.

In modern Western societies the speech patterns of men (vocal, dominant and direct) are seen as the norm by which women's speaking styles (collaborative, supportive and polite) are judged. Well-intentioned men speak to women as they would to other men: they "cut to the chase," are critical or even impolite, and feel little need to spare the feelings of their listener. They're bewildered when their words spark anger or resentment ("He's such a bully, I can't get a word in"). And women who talk like men (briefly, forcefully and interrupting) are judged harshly for coming across as rude or bitchy.

Given that in Western societies speaking (rather than listening) is considered the power position, it is no wonder that men interrupt and take the floor more often. And given that the purpose of women's conversation may be to enhance connection, it makes sense that women are much less likely to be "disrespectful" by interrupting.

Mansplaining

Author Rebecca Solnit first identified the concept in 2008, in a blog post entitled Men Explain Things To Me, in which she described an occasion when a man insisted on explaining a book to her, despite her trying to tell him that she had written it herself. (A later book of collected essays with the same title gave wider currency to the idea that men seemingly believe that no matter what a woman says, a man always knows better – which later came to be known as" Mansplaining".)

As prime minister, Teresa May exhibited low tolerance for it from male politicians, civil servants and journalists. And it was reported that being talked-over by her national security advisor Sir Mark Lyall Grant heralded his departure from Downing Street.

Manterrupting

Research on interrupting dates back to a small sample of conversations recorded at the University of California in 1975 which revealed that in 11 conversations between men and women, men interrupted 46 times, compared with women only twice.

Almost 40 years later things don't seem to have changed: a 2014 study at George Washington University found that when men were talking with women, they interrupted 33% more often than when talking with men. Women in the study rarely interrupted their male conversation partners (an average of once in a three-minute conversation).

Senior women get interrupted

Studies have found that male doctors interrupt their patients when they speak, especially female patients, but patients rarely interrupt their doctor – unless she is a woman. Women doctors make fewer interruptions, but are themselves interrupted more often. This is also true of corporate senior managers. Male bosses are seldom talked-over by the people who work for them, especially if the subordinate is a woman; however, female bosses are routinely interrupted by their male subordinates.

It happens to judges too. US research from the Pritzker School of Law found that over a 12-year period, 32% of interruptions were of women justices, despite the fact that they made up only 24% of the positions on the bench. Is it seniority, rather than gender which inhibits interruptions? Apparently not. Gender was three times more influential as a factor determining interruptions than seniority.

And it can happen in forums expressly addressing diversity issues. When Eric Schmidt, executive chairman of Google's parent company Alphabet, was participating in Q&A session following a panel discussion on corporate diversity, Google's own Global Diversity and Talent Program manager pointed out to him that Schmidt was repeatedly interrupting the only woman on the panel, who happened to be the Chief Technology Officer to the US government.

Even women favour women who talk less

The evidence shows that women hold back in discussions. You might think they become more forthright with seniority, when perhaps they're no longer deferring to men. But no.

At the Yale School of Management, Victoria Brescoll has examined the idea that the more senior a woman is, the more she makes a conscious effort to rein back her verbal contribution – the reverse of how most men handle power.

In the first of two experiments, men and women were asked to imagine themselves as either the most senior figure or the most junior in a meeting. Brescoll found that, unsurprisingly those men imagining themselves as senior said they would talk more than juniors, but women imagining they were senior said they would talk the same amount as the more junior women. Asked why, the women said they didn't want to be disliked, or to be seen as out of line.

In Brescoll's following experiment, men and women rated a fictitious female CEO who talked more than other people. The result: both sexes viewed this woman as significantly less competent and less suited to leadership than a male CEO who talked for the same amount of time. When the female CEO was described as talking *less* than others, her perceived competency shot up.

Girls are socialised to be polite

Women also tend to give way to interruptions in a way men don't, according to linguist Tannen, because of their socialisation to be polite. This means they talk less in mixed sex meetings. One of the Head Heart + Brain survey participants said: "At school I won a prize for 'manners'. Now I realise what that meant was that I kept quiet."

Girls are rewarded for taking turns, listening carefully, not swearing, being polite, and resisting interrupting – in ways we do not expect of boys. Boys' rowdy behaviour is dismissed as part of their nature, at least in Western culture. (There is some evidence that boys are expected to adopt a more polite and controlled manner in Asian societies.)

The advantages of women's speaking and listening style

Only when women are in the majority does a different pattern emerge. Ethan Burris from the McCombs School of Business studied employee vocalisation at a credit union where women made up 74% of supervisors and 84% of front-line employees. He found that when women spoke up there, they were more likely to be heeded than men.

Men and women are clearly socialised to communicate differently, which signals power relationships in workplace hierarchies, and as a result we often find colleagues set at odds with one another. But this inherent diversity could make for wider-ranging, more inclusive, more creative communications at work.

Women interrupt less, and appear to listen more: this could be encouraging a bottom-up communication of feedback and ideas. They themselves are interrupted more often: this could be less the manifestation of a lower status, and more a demonstration of an open and inclusive style. Burris has found this style generates more input from employees, harvesting more ideas and information about issues and how they could be resolved.

Women say important things – when we can hear them

A non-executive board member who contributed to the Head Heart + Brain research said that she noticed how often the women on the board were interrupted, whereas men were listened to without interruption. And women had less to say, but it tended to be more relevant to the topic under discussion. "I sometimes feel the men speak to remind you they are there, rather than to contribute to the debate or solving the issue," she said.

And a male MD of a retail company told us that when his management committee had a mix of men and women, the women came up with more and more useful ideas and had a perspective on employee and customer issues that men lacked.

This is supported by research carried out at Brigham Young University and Princeton which showed that, at a mixed table, women take up significantly less conversation time – 75% less than men – but the decisions made can be radically different if they depend on consensus-building. "When women participated more, they brought unique and helpful perspectives to the issue under discussion," says Chris Karpowitz from Brigham Young. "We're not just losing the voice of someone who would say the same things as everybody else in the conversation."

A new structure for meetings

The results of this study suggest that adopting a more structured approach to meetings, and particularly to decision-making, could reap benefits – particularly when women are outnumbered by men. One approach which has the advantage of tackling several issues at once is Nancy Kline's Thinking Environment which values, encourages and celebrates deep quality thinking.

From our discussions with Kline, it seems to be getting remarkable results. It includes a safe, inclusive environment as part of its design, and its 10 components also work according to the brain-savvy principles of minimising threat and increasing reward.

Kline's method helps to mitigate gender bias in two ways:

> • It encourages the masculine trait of thinking deeply and makes it accessible to both genders.
> • The principal behaviours used are mainly feminine in style and the process enables men to legitimately adopt these traits by providing an environment where they are not just required but celebrated.

These two components have an equalising effect, allowing men and women to practise a wider range of behaviours. The structured process also discourages any negative micro-behaviours, aggressive language or stealing of other people's ideas. It slows down thinking: going deeper, looking for quality over quantity, listening equally to everyone involved. And with some regular practice the process spreads throughout an organisation. Along the way the structured approach creates an environment where people do their best thinking and are equally heard.

Career hacks

Quick comebacks

If you're interrupted for any reason other than a brief request for clarification, have some prepared responses ready:

> "There are a few more essential points I need to make. Could you delay a moment while I do that? "
> "I know your feedback will be invaluable – can you hold that idea until I'm done?"
> "I think that's what I said – if you're disagreeing with me, just let me finish and then I'd like to hear your points."

Or if a man is co-opting your proposal:

> "I'm pleased you agree."
> "Interesting you say that, it's the point I made a few minutes ago."

When making these comebacks, keep your tone light and unemotional even if what you really want to say is, "You knucklehead, that's my idea!"

Watch your language

Some key points to help you communicate more powerfully and effectively (men can make use of them too):

Avoid gendered language: "Today, the typical graduate has no idea what he wants to do for a career" can be rephrased as "Today, most graduates struggle to make a career choice." Call out gendered language wherever you hear it.

Be concise: If you know you tend to ramble, particularly when nervous, practise keeping your phrasing succinct and don't go off at tangents: this helps to avoid interruptions. Make a list of key points you can glance at as you speak.

Avoid apologising: Avoid phrases like "Maybe I'm wrong, but..." Or "This is just my opinion..." They discredit what follows and suggest a lack of confidence. Ask someone who is regularly in meetings with you for feedback, then set an intention to change your language.

Do soften the impact: When you remove the hedging phrases like "I just," "I only, " "I may be wrong but..." from your vocabulary, be careful not to get rid of "softening language" altogether, particularly if you're dealing with other women. If you're dealing with a sensitive situation, practise using language that softens the impact without devaluing what you're saying. Like, "I have a view on this, but I'd also like to hear what you think." Or "Given we all seem to agree, as a first step we could..."

Make statements rather than ask questions: Women phrase an opinion as a question because it's a "safer" way to say what they want. For example, "What do you think about trying...?" or "Maybe we could...?" Instead, make questions actually questions, and your statements actually statements. If you're concerned about sounding too aggressive, try adding "I'd love to hear your feedback on this idea" after you've clearly expressed your thoughts.

Know when to be quiet: State your point briefly and clearly – then be quiet. Silence gives others a chance to consider what you've said, and to form their response. And silence can be helpful in establishing your credibility. One research participant reported how she kept quiet in her first few board meetings, making sure she understood the issues and the politics. When she did ask a question, it was on point, insightful and established her competence, and for the men was a bit of a wake-up call.

Act strategically

Pick your seat carefully: In meetings, sit where you can be both seen and heard: don't hang back, even if the room is full. Politely ask for room to be made at the table.

Lean in – literally: Follow the findings of the study which Sheryl Sandberg took for the title of her book, which revealed that men physically lean in more often than women in professional meetings, making them less likely to be interrupted. So: lean in, look directly at people, scan the room if it's a group meeting, and speak with conviction.

Use body language: Gesture towards someone, stand up, walk to the front of the room, place your hand on the table – whatever it takes. These expansive gestures and movements make you appear more authoritative, and research suggests they make you feel more confident as well (see Chapter 14).

Prep your nodder: It's immensely helpful to have someone onside in a meeting, nodding and looking interested when you speak. Set up a buddy system with a colleague, brief them on your proposal and ask them to back you up.

Interrupt the interrupter: Nudge them, put a hand on their arm, or simply speak up to say, "Hang on, can we let her finish," or "Oh, I'd like to hear what x is saying before we move on…" Find your own words - but don't stay silent.

Give credit where it's due: Everyone wants credit for a useful insight or a good idea. Research shows that giving credit where it's due, will actually make you look better (as well as the person with the idea). Do it for both men and women, but make sure you don't miss out the women. "I thought that was a really useful idea." "I really like the way Siobhan put that point."

Siobhan has been reading up on the effects of gendered language and now proposes alternative phrasing whenever it crops up. It's become a bit of a joke in the office, but one that everyone's joining in on and people are starting to pre-empt her corrections.

She has become more conscious and deliberate in her speaking style and when presenting: when she makes a point she doesn't introduce it apologetically, keeps her contributions short and to the point but makes sure she isn't interrupted. Her boss has mentioned she seems to be making more of a contribution.

Nikhil has been surprised by the research on male/female speaking styles. Since he doesn't really feel comfortable with his sometimes overbearing male colleagues he's taking care not to manterrupt and is making a point of being more supportive of his colleagues' contributions – especially the women. He's acknowledging their ideas and listening to the tone and the words: it's helping him to focus on what people are actually saying in meetings, rather than just trying to find a moment to make his own contribution.

Exploring further

Books

You Just Don't Understand: Woman and Men in Conversation, Deborah Tannen

The Power of Talk: Who Gets Heard and Why, Deborah Tannen

Men Explain Things to Me, Rebecca Solnit

Time to think: Listening to Ignite the Human Mind, Nancy Kline

Articles, blogs and podcasts

Are Women the Silent Sex? Tali Mendelberg and Christopher Karpowitz (The authors summarise their book.) Boston Review

Breaking Down the Problem with Mansplaining (and other forms of privileged explaining), R Nithya, Everyday Feminism

Men Who Explain Things, Rebecca Solnit (Mansplaining in action.) Los Angeles Times

A Gentleman's Guide to Mansplaining and Manterrupting, Dale Thomas Vaughan. (How to avoid being an accidental jerk.) The Good Men Project

Female Supreme Court Justices are interrupted more by Male Justices and Advocates, Tonja Jacobi and Dylan Schweers, Harvard Business Review

Women Get Interrupted More – Even By Other Women, Alice Robb (Both men and women seem to feel that women are "interruptible".) New Republic

Videos and webinars

What is Mansplaining? (A basic guide.) YouTube (3:24).

Mansplaining – the Science (A lightning-fast review of its prevalence.) YouTube (1:47).

"Girl" vs. "Woman": Why Language Matters, Mayim Bialik. (You don't call a grown man a "boy". How to change how we talk about women.) YouTube (4:04).

Gender-specific language rituals, Deborah Tannen (Videos of competitive language styles.) YouTube (8:02)

How to speak up when you feel like you can't, Adam Galinsky (Research and helpful tips on how to find your voice when it matters most, and how to advocate for others who need it.) TEDx (15:03)

Thinking Environment, Cheryl Reynolds. (Animated video of Nancy Kline's 10 components of the thinking environment, with examples of why they are important.) YouTube (7:09)

The Ten Components in the business environment. Nancy Kline (The author's speech *The Two Worlds of Thinking* invites coaches to dwell on "a tiny /huge question" which she believes differentiates extraordinary coaching from the mundane. YouTube (4:37)

5.
Who's doing the office housework

Siobhan has just finished her online grocery shopping (her partner didn't manage to do it – again). She feels as though she spends a lot of her working day looking after other people: training the graduate entrants, hand-holding clients, finessing the final arrangements for a day conference. And then she ends up doing most of the home-keeping as well. She asks Nikhil how much of this "office housework" he does.

He looks a little abashed: he was advised early on by one of the senior guys in his team not to take on extras like mentoring the graduate trainees or getting stuck with fetching the coffees for a meeting. So his tactic is only to do the things that get noticed by the people who matter. He'll offer to do the minutes if it gets him to a meeting he wouldn't normally be invited to; he'll get the drinks if it's for a senior leader he wouldn't usually get to meet.

Back in 1977 Harvard professor Rosabeth Moss Kanter observed that women do most of what she termed the "office housework": administrative tasks that help the business run smoothly but aren't part of their job role; things like taking notes, serving on committees and planning meetings, coaching and mentoring juniors.

Everyone loves the "office housekeeper" who tends to the smooth running of the organisation. But while they are doing these activities women are using up their time and energy, and missing out on more powerful opportunities. The person working late in the office to catch up after coaching a newbie hardly ever gets noticed. Or rewarded. Or promoted. This isn't a skill set that will enhance your performance evaluation. (In fact, there are several studies that suggest it can harm you, especially if women call a halt to the work overload it causes.)

Yes, the housekeepers are women.

Examining the growth of collaborative work in business, researchers from the University of Pennsylvania Wharton School established that up to 35% of this work is typically done by 3% to 5% of employees who, not surprisingly, often become overloaded and experience burn-out. And who are these super-collaborators? Yes, they're women. Women end up with the "lion's share" of collaborative work, according to Adam Grant, Reb Rebele and Rob Cross, and they're less likely to get credit for helping their colleagues than their male peers.

Within even the most macho professions this kind of paying-attention-to helps to oil the wheels, but it always seems to fall to women. Women are socialised to help others, to notice what is required and to smile while they take on the little extras. In work this translates to being a team player. The assumption is that women like being supportive, and that they're better at it. Siobhan recalls one of her colleagues grumbling when she was asked to do the guided tour for interns – again – and one of the guys asking what was the big deal: she was good at doing this kind of stuff, and she'd done it before so she knew the ropes.

Men are lauded, women are expected

Just as at home, when a man may be lauded just for taking the recycling out, or cooking one meal a week, so it is at work. New York University psychologist Madeline Heilman conducted a study that asked participants to rate men and women employees who did or did not stay late to help colleagues prepare for a big meeting the next day. When both agreed to stay late, the man was rated 14% more favourably than the woman. When both refused, the woman was rated 12% lower than the man, even though they had done exactly the same thing.

"Over and over, after giving identical help, a man was significantly more likely to be recommended for promotions, important projects, raises and bonuses," says Heilman. "A woman had to help just to get the same rating as a man who didn't help."

Women are expected to be nurturing and helpful, while men are expected to be ambitious and results-oriented – but if he lends a hand as well he's praised and rewarded. And when a man says he can't help because he's "busy" that's understandable, but when a woman says no she isn't a team player.

Re-classifying housework

Helpful work is invisible and unrewarded, noticed only when it's not done or done badly. One way to give women the credit they deserve for it is to re-classify it: give it a new name and a new status and change it from being a nice-to-do of no great value, to being as important to the work men do as it is to the work women are expected to do.

UCLA psychologist Shelley Taylor proposed the term "tending" (which she believed had the benefit of being gender-neutral). She used it to describe the many relationship-enhancing activities that happen among colleagues at work to promote social connection and collaboration.

Taylor demonstrated the value of tending behaviour, showing how an action as simple as the boss stopping by at everyone's desk to say, "good morning" reduces stress and its associated emotional, physical, and social impact. Mentoring (a classic act of workplace tending) improves skills, brings on people with potential, increases job opportunities and job satisfaction, and reduces staff turnover. Tending behaviour increases productivity, Taylor says.

Her terminology may not have caught on, but the advantage of re-framing this work is to raise its profile and the recognition of its importance to the smooth-running of an organisation – which can prompt senior leaders to reward it.

Writing in the New York Times in 2015, Sheryl Sandberg and Adam Grant opt for Kanter's term "office housework" to describe this type of discretionary work. They point to the research that shows organisations with cultures that encourage these collaborative behaviours have better business results, including better levels of sales, profits and customer satisfaction. They also highlight that women are more likely to feel emotionally exhausted. In doing the lion's share, it seems women often sacrifice themselves.

Top-down change

A small number of CEOs recognise the problem. CEO Sharon

Rowlands, of US software company ReachLocal, makes a point of distributing office housework, such as note-taking, on a strict rotation that includes everyone, regardless of seniority.

Virgin Group founder Richard Branson, who willingly takes the notes in meetings, says the unequal distribution of this work is "unfair to women, but it's also disadvantageous to men. It's time for men to step up and do their share of support work. On top of counteracting gender bias in the work force, it will also give men a better understanding of what is going on within the business and what needs to be done to make things run more effectively."

Push back and share the load

If you feel you're overloaded and the cause is too much "housework", start by examining your mind-set: if we want to help others, we need to take care of ourselves first.

Wharton organisational psychologist Adam Grant says that women (and men) achieve their highest performance and experience the least burnout when they prioritise their own needs along with the needs of others. By putting the needs of other people before their own women are doing themselves harm. We know that helping other people creates a sense of reward in the brain. Women may feel less altruistic when they take care of themselves first, but they will be more influential, will be able to sustain energy and avoid exhaustion: ultimately, they can give more.

Consider how you can be smarter about the way the housework work gets done. If you are prepared to step in, make sure you're the organiser, not the do-er. Assign a junior to take the notes in a client meeting they would not normally get to attend. Instead of meeting one-on-one with mentees, invite them to lunch and get them to help each other and build their networks. Have an eye on the greater goal of recalibrating the "caring culture" of the office: set up a system (a Wiki page?) that shares the role around the whole team. And include the boss – think what a powerful message it sends if he's the person assigned to bake Julie's birthday cake in November.

And when someone makes an unreasonable request, instead of struggling to say you're too busy explain that it would stretch your team past breaking point. By explaining that you're protecting others, you can say no but still seem willing and supportive.

Career hacks

Smooth comebacks

If you're asked too often to do office housework practise these smooth responses.

The request to bring in the coffee/cakes/refreshments:

> "Do you realise how expensive that would make the cake given my hourly rate?"
>
> "Alice did the coffee run last time. Nikhil, you're up..."

To requests to buddy or mentor:

> "Nikhil I know one of your goals is to improve your relationship skills. This is the perfect opportunity."
>
> "Women are great at this stuff anyway; I don't want you to miss this opportunity to be seen as helping the new intake."

When repeatedly asked to take notes, or arrange meetings:

> "You know, it would be good practice for one of the juniors and they'll get valuable experience observing the client meeting. I'll get Sanjay to come."
>
> "Logistics is an essential skill for us: do you want to ask the new graduate to get familiar with the meeting set-up software"?
>
> "If Richard Branson can take the notes in his meetings I think we can all take a turn. Harry why don't you start the rota?"

Saying no

Sometimes you just have to say No. And one of the best ways to give yourself the determination to say No is to be clear about what you are saying Yes to. What is the more important thing you're giving your time or energy to (like a client's report, or the performance review of a talented employee, or your own wellbeing).

Saying why you can't do the task requested helps the person making the request understand your priorities and preserves the relationship. Taking it one step further and making a suggestion about how to get the task done, though not by you, is even more helpful.

Siobhan realises the reason she says yes to "office housework" is because she's empathetic – but it's not doing her any favours. Having a more strategic approach, helping others help themselves eases her workload but still means the office runs smoothly and she feels helpful and she avoids being dumped-on.

She feels more in control now that she's decided it's important to prioritise her own needs, and she's found ways to delegate the office housework which still lets her feel she's a valued contributor

Exploring further

Books

The Tending Instinct: Women, Men, and the Biology of our Human Relationships, Shelley Taylor

Give and Take, Adam Grant

Articles, blogs and podcasts

The Office Mom, Laura Sinberg (The advantages of bringing emotional warmth into the corporate world.) forbes.com

Madam CEO Get Me a Coffee, Sheryl Sandberg and Adam Grant (Women doing the "office housework.") New York Times

Office Housework Gets in Women's Way, Deborah Kolb and Jessica Porter (Four strategies for saying No to the office housework.) Harvard Business Review.

Videos and webinars

Gender Equality is Making Men Feel Discriminated Against (How gender equality is shaping men's political views.) Harvard Business Review (2:23)

Women Doing "Office Housework"? Barb Bartlein (Discussion of a New York Times article which proposed that in workplaces "women help more but benefit less from it".) You Tube (6:13)

6.
Are you paid less because "women don't negotiate"?

We now introduce you to Matt and Louise, who are facing the different career challenges that come with seniority. Louise has been at Multinational Trading for five years. She took on a new role six months ago and was delighted to get more responsibility, but was told she would have to wait until the next pay round to receive a pay increase. She's just found out that she's earning 20% less than her friend and colleague Matt. He was recruited externally at the same time as she was promoted: it seems that because he came from outside he wasn't affected by the pay date rules. Is this what "the gender pay gap" looks like?

Louise regrets not fighting for a pay rise when she was promoted, especially as she's good at negotiating with clients, and on behalf of her team. Should she have challenged the pay rules? Would there have been any fallout if she had?

Is it true that women are hopeless at negotiating their salaries and have low expectations of their worth? Or could it be that the internal policies of organisations work differently for women than men?

Fix women or fix the system?

Professor of economics at Carnegie Mellon, Linda Babcock, has found that amongst business-school graduates men initiate salary negotiations four times as often as women do, and that when women do negotiate, they ask for 30% less money than men.

At Manchester Business School, Marilyn Davidson has seen the same pattern, and believes that it stems from a lack of confidence. Each year she asks her students what they expect to earn, and what they deserve to earn five years after graduation. "I've been doing this for about seven years," she says, "and every year there are massive differences between the male and female responses." On average, she reports, the men think they deserve £80,000 a year and the women £64,000: a massive 20% less.

One woman respondent in the Head Heart + Brain survey backed up Louise's experience. She told us: "It seems more common for women to progress internally and be appointed to fixed salary points, while more men seem to be recruited from outside the company and can negotiate their compensation." What was needed to redress the situation, she suggested, was the opportunity to negotiate salary on promotion.

Women *also* have to negotiate social acceptance

A Columbia Business School study has found that while women do worse than men in economic negotiations, including salary negotiations, women do not lack the skills or motivation to bargain effectively. Rather, women are simultaneously negotiating social approval in the light of gender role expectations which lead them to not being assertive in some contexts, such as when bargaining for themselves.

However they *are* good at negotiating on behalf of others. The researchers believe this is because in this context the bargaining is viewed as caring and therefore consistent with a feminine stereotype.

The research involved a survey of executives' experiences in the workplace, as well as laboratory re-creations of salary negotiations for themselves and on behalf of other people. The survey responses showed that women did not in fact aspire to lower salaries than men; they also did not aspire to higher targets when they were bargaining on behalf of other people rather than themselves. So lower aspirations do *not* appear to be the reason for women's lower negotiation outcomes. Instead, the results suggest that the reason for women's lower outcomes is concern about the social impact of the negotiation on themselves.

When women were bargaining for others they were strong advocates and held the line in negotiations, but when bargaining on their own behalf their behaviour altered: they were much less demanding. (This was only seen with women – the men did not alter their behaviour.) When bargaining for themselves female negotiators made larger concessions: nearly 20% of the total value of the salary in the first round. This was greater than the concessions made by male negotiators, or by men or women bargaining on behalf of others.

Why was this? The research supports the argument that women negotiating for money and resources in the workplace are simultaneously "negotiating" social approval, and this accounted for their stereotyped behaviour. And other experiments in the study suggest that this adaptability is (unfortunately) wise: observers are more likely to form negative impressions of women who are bargaining strongly for themselves. The Columbia researchers say their work shows women are *not* unskilled in negotiations, but social expectations (which they clearly recognise and effectively adapt to) prevent them bargaining hard for themselves.

So what needs changing is the overall context of the negotiations.

Including social outcomes in hard bargaining

Another piece of research from Harvard and Carnegie Mellon suggests women must weigh the benefits of negotiating against the social consequences. To address this dilemma, the authors tested two strategies to help women improve both their negotiation and social outcomes in compensation negotiations.

In one study, factoring in concern for organisational relationships in the negotiation helped the evaluation of the women: they experienced less negative ratings. In the phase of the study where women gave a legitimate rationale for why they should receive the higher salary they got the compensation they desired. However, neither strategy - alone or in combination - improved both women's social *and* negotiation outcomes.

In a second study, the researchers tested another two strategies devised to improve female negotiators' social and financial outcomes, by explaining why a compensation request is legitimate in relational terms. For example, by explaining the impact on their standing with colleagues as well as the value of their skills and experience in the market. Results showed that the best strategy for women, that didn't rock the boat of gender stereotyping but which got them the financial reward they deserved, was to highlight the benefits to the wider group as well as explaining the rationale for the increase.

Advocacy for others rather than assertiveness

Emily Amanatullah, who led the Columbia Business School study, says, "The present results suggest a different remedy than training female negotiators to behave assertively. Training programmes should focus on role shifting. It may be fruitful to teach female negotiators how to reframe self-advocacy negotiations as situations of other-advocacy."

For example, the researchers propose that when negotiating her salary, a woman might frame it as bargaining on behalf of her family, or helping the organisation meet particular goals. When negotiating budgets at work, a female manager might frame her actions as bargaining on behalf of her division or team.

In addition, women can propose swapping negotiation roles with each other to avoid self-advocacy. Enlightened organisations might quite rightly consider whether it's right that financial rewards should depend on hard-headed, essentially selfish bargaining skills. Instead, one woman could ask another to make the case for her pay rise, and she could reciprocate. How practical these suggestions are will vary from one organisation to another, but for women in the bargaining seat the key message, if you want to maintain social standing *and* get the money, is to avoid sounding selfish (which goes against the ingrained stereotype). And think of why what you want helps other people or the organisation.

Negotiations are an emotional process

This is not just how women experience negotiations: it's part of our neurological wiring. Neuroscientist Antonio Damasio made a ground-breaking discovery when studying patients with damage in the amygdala where emotions are generated. Outwardly, the patients all seemed to function normally, except for their inability to feel emotions. They could describe what they should do in logical terms, but they all had something unexpected in common: they couldn't make decisions. These patients found it very difficult to decide even simple things like a time for their next appointment, or which restaurant they would have lunch in.

Damasio's conclusion was that even when we believe we are being driven by logic, decision-making is a profoundly emotional process. (This is an understanding which has had a significant impact on the work of professional mediators and negotiators.)

Pointers for better negotiations

Building on Damasio's work, and other neuroscience studies, mediation specialist Jeremy Lack and his co-negotiator François Bogacz suggest key "neuro-principles" that influence negotiation and dispute resolution situations. These principles are very similar to our Brain Basics in the introductory chapter to the other half of this book, and cover the importance of social connection, the impact of the threat and reward response in the brain and the impact of unconscious bias in decisions.

According to their work these neuro-principles have practical implications for the way negotiators can prepare, generate options, and gain agreement. Let's consider six of them:

1 Reduce any threat

As humans, our brains perceive threat three to five times more often than they react to reward. And feeling threatened can make us irrational because the executive functions of the brain are being hijacked by the emotional centres.

If you feel threat in a negotiation you may see the offer you're being made as completely unreasonable, or feel that the person you're negotiating with is jumping to conclusions. Or you may just get stuck on a single point and become obsessive about it, ignoring the bigger picture. Alternatively, you may go into flight mode and withdraw and give in, or you yourself may be triggered to fight back.

It's important to minimise the threat for yourself, and the person you're negotiating with. Start with a handshake. Acknowledge that there may need to be a bit of hard bargaining to be done, but you hope you can both keep focused on what's important. Identify what you've both got in common. And if things get a bit heated suggest taking a break. The key is to make human connection and not to let the heat of the bargaining impact the relationship.

2 Our responses are biased

Given that decisions are based on emotions, all our information is filtered through our thought habits, and the stories we tell ourselves. We also know that our brain takes shortcuts which can result in bias. This can play a role in how negotiations unfold, from escalating a belief that the issues under negotiation are all fixed, to underestimating an offer, to making assumptions about an offer which aren't verified. For example, a second offer appears to be relatively more valuable if it's made after a very low first offer.

Other common biases at play are:

• Initial proposals can become set in stone, and a desire for consistency prevents negotiators from changing them. (The figure you came up with for your proposed annual bonus, which you were prepared to negotiate, somehow becomes a deal-breaker for you.) This desire for consistency is often exacerbated by a desire to save face or to maintain an impression of expertise or control. (No-one likes to give in, especially when the other party may see it as a weakness.)

• As a negotiator you may approach the bargaining as a win-or-lose exchange. It's hard to imagine a compromise which has benefits for both sides. In this state of mind you may fail to look for the mutual benefits or respond to suggestions, and this leads you to ignore or to not give enough consideration to concessions that may have been made by the other person. ("We can meet your salary expectations but not the job title. Can the role be called…")

• The very offer of a proposal from someone such as senior manager, or a human resources manager you don't know and trust, who is by definition in your out-group, may seem suspicious: "Where's the catch?"

• Amos Tversky and Daniel Kahneman, the Israeli psychologists who are the founders of behavioural economics, coined the phrase "loss aversion" to describe our tendency to strongly prefer avoiding losses to acquiring gains. This explains why, when you have invested in something (either emotionally, financially or with your time) you find it difficult to make decisions that would result in any loss.

In a negotiation you might resist an offer because it involves losing something you created. A good example might be tolerating poor performance of a team member: the loss of your investment in that person makes you less likely to make a decision about dealing with their poor performance. Taking a step back and considering *why* you are rejecting an offer, or running the situation past a colleague, helps to bring the bias to the surface.

3 The power of nudges

As we mentioned in the chapter on influence (Chapter 7 in the other half of the book), the use of words or behaviour to direct the mind can be highly influential, not least in negotiations. Even the use of a single word – like *keep* instead of *lose* – in the presentation of options can unconsciously influence the conscious choices people make.

This is a good tactic to remember when negotiating on money, resources or role-responsibilities. Say "I want to keep all the people responsibilities of my current role," rather than "I don't want to lose all the interesting parts of my current job."

Framing, which is how you set up the negotiation ("This is an opportunity for us both to achieve our desired outcomes") or reformulating ("I would rather think of this as an exploration of what we can achieve together rather than a negotiation") are also important, as they offer ways to shape how initial patterns of behaviour and negotiations unfold.

It's also important to consider non-verbal communications that may influence the negotiation, like where you sit and your level of friendliness. People tend to trust warmer people. Your body language should be inviting connection: are you smiling when you greet the person you're bargaining with, leaning in, and listening carefully?

It's worth considering these points before you get started. Your pre-meeting preparation sets up a perception of your strength, for example if you "prime" by requesting copies of your business unit's profit and loss statement, or the organisation's formal salary or gender policy, you look serious and prepared without being hostile. Mediator Jeremy Lack talks about negotiations not simply as a facilitated agreement process but a facilitated social, emotional and cognitive process.

4 Fairness is profoundly important to us

Equity is a need for men and women: we have an innate drive to reject perceived unfairness, but this can get in the way of other innate instincts for social connection and being accommodating. Our need for fairness drives behaviour as much as our need to be accepted by people who are important to us, like our boss. Our success in a salary negotiation, or any negotiations (as in all human life) rests on our ability to manage the balance between cooperation and self-interest.

More than three decades of research show that humans are prepared to reject unfair offers even at a personal cost. These studies commonly use the "ultimatum game" in which one person gets an amount of money – say, £10 – and proposes a split with a second person, such as £9 for herself, £1 for the other person. If the second person decides to reject the offer they both get nothing.

The results consistently show that despite the offer of "free money", about half the time the second person rejects any offer of less than 25% of the total. Even though a bit of money is worth more than none, what may be seen as an insultingly small share is rejected: the sense of unfairness devalues the monetary value.

What this means in terms of your pay negotiation is if you perceive an offer to be unfair you are likely to react strongly. It may be best to take a step back and to consider your options: would you prefer a small, unfair raise or no raise at all? Or does the unfairness of the offer so offend you that you're willing to take other action, like looking for a new job?

And if your boss believes that most women have a partner who is the major breadwinner you may find that what seems fair to them may look very different to you. Neuroscience shows that perceptions of "fairness" are highly subjective. It's worth trying to understand where they're coming from to anticipate their negotiating tactics and offers.

5 If you're prepared to be accommodating, be surprising!

While unfairness may create discord, it's not in human nature to hold a grudge until the other side capitulates. Research shows we're highly motivated to cooperate when it's for the greater good, even when it may not be in our immediate best interest. (The organisation is going through lean times / there's a need for salary sacrifice to enable capital investment...) Behavioural stereotypes suggest that women will be particularly good at this: women tend to cooperate and collaborate.

Women who are accommodating when they negotiate are often branded as weak or gullible, but you have a choice when it's your salary at stake: negotiate hard and risk a backlash, or be accommodating but poorer!

If you *are* prepared to be flexible in a salary negotiation for the good of the organisation (and can afford to be), there's evidence to show that the power of a conciliatory gesture lies in it being unexpected. (According to dozens of imaging studies, the brain gets a greater sense of reward from the positive unexpected rather than the positive expected.) So, don't create an image of yourself as the easy pushover. Go in well-prepared to negotiate strongly. Then if you're prepared to concede on salary or key benefits, make the proposal yourself. The element of surprise is yours, and appears to come from a position of strength.

6 Setting yourself up for success

The way the brain responds in negotiations suggests it is very important to be well-prepared and to signal to the person you are negotiating with that you can be both tough and collaborative, that you value them and their point of view and have taken time to understand it.

You need to take into account three things: human tendencies and how they might influence negotiation; how our own perceptions influence outcomes; and how the process itself can trigger impressions that we don't check. These affect everyone's behaviour and willingness to make concessions and accept offers.

Finally, negotiating to achieve your goals while maintaining your accepted social standing means thinking carefully about how you frame your arguments to be about the good of the organisation or the group. You need to decide whether you will follow the stereotype and be collaborative and accommodating, or ignore all that and do what's most beneficial to you.

Career hacks

Managing the size of a problem

Negotiations can feel risky, we worry and build up concerns in our mind. "Will I fail to convince…" "What if they only offer…." When we see something as risky or we lack confidence and this lack of confidence in our ability to get the right outcome, distorts reality. Problems seem bigger, darker and more insurmountable then they really are.

When you are feeling concerned by a negotiation or by a task or issue follow the steps below to gain control and increase confidence.

Think about the negotiation. Notice how you see it in your mind's eye:

- Notice the colours, how light or dark it is
- The size of the picture in your mind
- How far or close it is to you?
- Are there any sounds? Are they soothing or harsh? (There may be no sound)
- What are the feelings that accompany the picture in your mind?

Now shake off that image. Shift position.

Now think about something that is good or joyful. Again, notice how you see this in your mind's eye using the questions above. Enjoy the image for a little while.

Shake off the image. Makes some notes of the differences you noticed.

Now go back to the negotiation or problem. Recreate the image in your minds eye. Gradually transfer the characteristics from the joyful image into the negotiation image.

- Make the colours, and light the same
- Move the position
- Add or take away the sound
- Add or take way the feelings

Keep playing with each aspect until this image has the same characteristics as the good image you saw. Notice how you feel about the negotiation now: less concerned, more confident. If anything needs adjusting go back and make changes until it feels manageable, you are confident in your abilities and the outcome you can achieve.

On reflection, Louise realises she didn't do her homework on comparative earnings in the organisation, and gave away her opportunity to negotiate when she was promoted. She was a bit of a pushover; it's a tough lesson for the future.

She's going to put herself forward for more responsibility in negotiations with clients and suppliers, and use the insights she's learned in her next pay negotiation.

Exploring further

Books

Women Don't Ask, Linda Babcock (By failing to negotiate her starting salary for her first job, a woman may sacrifice over a half a million pounds in earnings by the end of her career.)

Articles, blogs and podcasts

The Business Case for Gender Pay Gap Transparency, Business in the Community. (Factsheet making the case for why more employers should publish their gender pay data.) bitc.org.uk

Women, Work and the State of Work Inequality 2017, Jessica Kirkpatrick (Research by US-based employment agency into gender bias and the expectation gap.) hired.com

Videos and webinars

Negotiation: Getting What You Want, Margaret Neale (Negotiation is problem solving. The goal is not to get a deal; the goal is to get a good deal.) Stanford Business School (24:36)

20% Counts – See What 20% Looks Like, leanin.org (A humorous video: what life is like when you get 20% less... of everything.) YouTube (1:45)

#Equal Future – Pocket Money, ANZ Bank. (Kids were asked to do some chores; the girls were paid less than the boys: just like in the real world.) YouTube (1:31)

Two Monkeys Were Paid Unequally: Excerpt from Frans de Waal's TED Talk. (The response to blatant unfairness) YouTube (2:43)

Why you should know how much your coworkers get paid, David Burkus (How much do you get paid? How does it compare to the people you work with? Management researcher Burkus makes a compelling case for why sharing information could benefit employees, organisations and society.) TED.com (7:29)

Know your worth, and then ask for it, Casey Brown. (Your boss probably isn't paying you what you're worth – they're paying you what they think you're worth. Take the time to learn how to shape their thinking.) TED.com (8:22)

7.
Your confidence and career sabotage

Louise is having a crisis of confidence. Despite a recent promotion to team manager she's had feedback from her boss that she needs to be more confident and project a more authoritative image: she should speak up more with clients, put herself forward, and stamp her mark on her team. She gets the impression she was almost promoted despite herself. The message is that she now has to take charge of her career.

Louise feels it's all very well being told she needs to be more confident, but adopting masculine bluster and bigging-herself-up doesn't sit well with her. Matt doesn't really understand her concerns: her performance ratings are the same as his and she has a reputation for very strong technical knowledge. He suspects it's all in her head.

Over the years, we women have kept our heads down and played by what we believed were the rules: we've believed that hard work and natural talent would be recognised and rewarded. After a 30-plus year career one of your authors (Jan) can see there has been some progress, but neither of us want to see change continuing at this snail's pace so that Francesca is still facing similar issues when she reaches the same stage in her career.

The bigger picture

Men continue to get promoted faster and to be paid more. Research in the UK in 2017 by consulting firm Pipeline found that in FTSE 350 companies only 16% of executive committee members were women, and women accounted for only 6% of all executives who had profit and loss responsibility (as opposed to running functions like marketing or HR).

Both of these figures had not changed over the previous year. And the trend is not going in the right direction on boards either. The number of FTSE 350 companies with *no* women on their boards actually increased to 60 (an additional eight companies in the year) and the number of companies with no female executives with financial responsibility increased to 147 (an increase of 16 in the year.)

These numbers make no sense in the context of the study that also found the companies which have at least 25% female executives had net profit margins that were on average double those of companies who had no women executives in these senior positions.

The statistics are similar in the rest of the world: at the top, especially, there are very few women. In the US, McKinsey's Women in the Workplace 2015 research predicts that it will take 100 years for gender equality to be achieved. The ease and pace of career progression for women is very different from men.

Are we self-sabotaging?

Numerous theories are bandied about to explain the lack of progress on gender equality. And many of them point the finger at women themselves. Women take time out to raise children, for example – though this doesn't explain the lack of progress for women who don't have children. Women don't reach for the top because they are not ambitious. Or, yes, they just lack confidence and fail to put themselves forward.

This is "Fix the Women" thinking, and it has driven an industry of coaching and corporate gender initiatives for the last 15 years. We women just need to take ourselves in hand, rearrange our ideas, go on some courses and man-up, and we will progress right up through the glass ceiling. The constraints upon us, it's assumed, are essentially internal, and a kind of self-sabotage.

Fix the women

Companies have addressed the issue with women's networks (where women can help each other), women's leadership training, mentoring and coaching, especially as they return to the workplace after parental leave. And our research participants told us they had benefited from many of these initiatives, but none of them had the effect of consistently moving the dial on their careers, or the careers of other women in the company.

One issue seems to be that organisations approach the problem piecemeal: they try one thing, get minimal results, abandon it and try something else. (More about how to create lasting change in Chapter 16, Building a gender-savvy organisation, in this half of the book.)

So, do women sabotage their own careers? It's an idea that deserves examination, because – of course – for as long as the barriers to women's career progression seem to be essentially individual and personal, it takes the focus away from men needing to change their attitudes and behaviour, or any kind of industry-wide, structural change.

But as we have said in the introduction because this is a book that focuses on neurological and psychological insights, rather than industrial or political campaigning, we'll be looking at how the beliefs about women and their confidence that frame our reality, stack up against the research. And we'll look at the practical steps we ourselves can take to address the current beliefs.

Let's look at three major issues: the self-sabotaging "imposter syndrome"; whether women do actually lack confidence or just don't demonstrate it in the same way as men; and how overtly-confident women may attract a hostile reaction.

1 "I'm an imposter" syndrome

One of the major issues women are said to contend with is "imposter syndrome". You'll have heard it referred to by high-achieving individuals, both men and women, being asked to account for their success.

British author Neil Gaiman says he used to have elaborate fantasies of someone knocking on his door to make him stop writing and get a real job. Actor Jodie Foster has said she thought she'd be asked to give her Oscar back.

Sheryl Sandberg has recalled attending a Harvard University address titled "Feeling Like a Fraud" and thinking that every remark was directed personally at her —she'd fooled them all. She said in an article for The Cut: "Every time I was called on in class, I was sure that I was about to embarrass myself. Every time I took a test, I was sure that it had gone badly. And every time I didn't embarrass myself — or even excelled — I believed that I had fooled everyone yet again."

In an article for Leanin.org, Emma Walmsley, CEO for GSK, says that every time in her 17-year career she was offered big promotions she always came home and told her husband she couldn't do it. (And he would remind her that she did always succeed.)

Is imposter syndrome real?

There may well be an element of self-deprecation and charming modesty here – after all, no-one looks attractive saying "I always knew I was going to be great."

But this is a more substantial phenomenon first observed in 1978 by psychologist Pauline Rose Clance at the college where she was teaching in Ohio. She noted that many of the accomplished female students demonstrated the same self-beliefs: despite their strong academic track records, these women felt that they didn't deserve their success. They attributed their achievements to luck, or a mistake, and felt sure that they would be "found out". Many went so far as to say that their acceptance into the college had been a mistake which the administrators would soon realise and they would be asked to leave.

It sounds outlandish but the evidence she presented in *The Impostor Phenomenon in High Achieving Women* was persuasive. Her theory was that women are uniquely predisposed to the impostor phenomenon because success for women does not match society's expectations or women's own internalised self-evaluations. Clance later devised a scale which rated people on how they responded to statements such as "It's hard for me to accept compliments or praise about my intelligence or accomplishments," "At times, I feel my success has been due to some kind of luck," and "I often compare my ability to those around me and think they may be more intelligent than I am."

The women who agreed most strongly tended to attribute their success to some quirk of personality, or factors outside of themselves (to luck, or the good fortune of having a very supportive partner). In our own research, women told us they were "in the right place at the right time". One senior civil servant put her success down to her different family background and education which she believed made her novel and noticeable.

Imposters are everywhere

There are now hundreds of articles and personal accounts on the theme of the imposter syndrome and it's frequently cited as one of the ways women sabotage their own careers: they just don't manage to believe in themselves. It's popularly understood today as a kind of internalised sexism, but that's not an idea which is supported by current research. In 1993 Clance conceded that imposter syndrome doesn't just affect women but that almost everyone suffers from it at times. We fall prey to it when we take on a new role, or a project goes wrong, or when we are having a difficult time at work.

Harvard Business School psychologist Amy Cuddy says in her book *Presence: Bringing Your Boldest Self to Your Biggest Challenges*, the reason imposter syndrome is identified more with women is simply that men are less likely to talk about these insecurities: they're aware of the social punishment that accompanies failing to live up to the stereotype of assertive and confident men.

The likeable imposter

Clance believes there may be advantages to experiencing the impostor syndrome: these people are likeable. "Most high-IP (Imposter Phenomenon) people that I have worked with are liked and respected and they're competent," she says. "The humility that IP people have can be appealing."

But beware the attraction of the humblebrag: it can become a self-perpetuating prophesy. If you maintain that you're a fraud and everyone else is highly competent, you may find ways to confirm that belief, attributing any success to luck even if it means discounting the evidence of achievements or performance reviews. (Which seems to be what Louise is doing just now.)

If every time you're preparing a presentation you're thinking that you don't really belong in this team (they're all so much smarter and more experienced than you are) in neurological terms you're reinforcing the circuitry of that self-doubt in your brain, and actually increasing the likelihood that you will mess up.

It's important to keep imposter syndrome in perspective. Everyone experiences it from time to time (particularly when starting new jobs), but women just talk about it more. A little self-doubt can add an edge, making sure you don't coast and preventing arrogance. But if you're getting too familiar with self-doubt remember what Bertrand Russell said: "The trouble with the world is that the stupid are cocksure and the intelligent are full of doubt."

2 Women lack confidence... or do they?

This is another way in which women are seen to be responsible for their own lack of career achievement: they don't project confidence in the same way that men do. It's not that they think they're imposters, but they hold back because they feel it's unseemly to push for the promotion, ask for a raise or speak up with a risky idea. It's "just not my style." One participant in the Head Heart + Brain survey commented: "Women's own preoccupations with what others think of them leads to a lack of confidence and hesitant behaviour, which reinforces stereotypes."

The popular beliefs are that, compared with men, women don't consider themselves as ready for promotions, they predict they'll do worse on tests, they are more risk-adverse, they wait until they are more skilled, and they generally underestimate their abilities.

But it seems we operate in a society dominated by over-confident bluffers. Work at Cornell University into cognitive bias resulted in the formulation in 1999 of the now-famous Dunning-Kruger effect describing the tendency for low-ability people to suffer from mistaken superiority. The research found that the less competent people were, the more they overestimated their abilities.

Subsequent research by David Dunning with Joyce Ehrlinger from Washington State University focused on women's confidence and competence. They wanted to test if a belief by women that they weren't that strong on science impacted their results in science tests.

Women underrate their skills

When men and women were asked to rate their own scientific skills, on average the women (as expected) rated themselves lower than the men. They then tested the participants on their scientific reasoning but before revealing the test results again asked participants to estimate how they had performed. The women's estimates were consistently lower than the men's, but their actual results were almost the same (women got 7.5 out of 10 questions right and the men 7.9)

To demonstrate the real-world impact of self-perception, the students were then invited – without knowing how they had performed – to participate in a science competition for prizes. The women were much more likely to turn down the opportunity: only 49% of them agreed to take part in the competition compared with 71% of the men. The researchers' conclusion was that women did not take up the opportunity because they were less confident.

This conclusion is fairly typical of the assumptions made by researchers interpreting this kind of data: women lack confidence. An alternative explanation might be that, without knowing how they had done, and given they underestimated their abilities, the women in the study quite rationally didn't want to waste their time or expose themselves to public ridicule.

Challenging the evidence

So, what is the evidence from business? The data most frequently referred to (including by Sheryl Sandberg and management consultants McKinsey) is internal research at Hewlett Packard which is said to have found that women applied for a promotion only when they believed they met 100% of the criteria listed for the job. Men were happy to apply when they thought they could meet 60% of the criteria.

This data has been referred to so frequently it has become a "truth": women hold back until they have the perfect experience, while underqualified men apply anyway. And indeed, several of the Head Heart + Brain research respondents offered examples of women having to be pushed to apply for roles they believed they were only partially qualified for. One senior HR director said that when she works with women going for promotions she's aware they are more likely to focus on their shortcomings than their accomplishments: "They believe the boss needs to think they're perfect before they dare ask for promotion." A senior woman in government told us: "In general women aren't as brazen as men and tend to think 'I can't do that' whereas a man thinks 'I can do most of that and I'll fake the rest of it.'"

But according to academic researcher Curt Rice, the HP story is just a story – not research. There may be data but it's not available for examination and we don't know how statistically significant it is. It appears this may have been an anecdote told to a McKinsey consultant during research at Hewlett Packard and subsequently quoted by Sandberg and others. It's not to say this is wrong: we just don't know if it's valid. But it's a potentially damaging assumption we seem to be ready to believe.

Conserving energy rather than under-confident

US women's development coach Tara Mohr was also sceptical of the conclusions from the HP data and carried out her own survey of around 1,000 American men and women professionals. She asked specifically, *"If you decided not to apply for a job because you didn't meet all the qualifications, why didn't you apply?"* According to self-reporting by her respondents, the barrier to applying was not lack of confidence but a lack of understanding how hiring and selection works.

Three of the reasons given by women, which together accounted for 78% of their responses, were to do with believing that the job qualifications were real requirements and seeing the hiring process as more by-the-book than it really is. If this is the case, women could be seen as more compliant (while men see the requirements more as a guideline and are prepared to take a chance and possibly bluff their way through). Or possibly women just don't want to (or can't afford to) waste time and energy on a long-shot.

The stories that hold us back

Qualifications have historically played a different role for women than for men. The 20th Century saw women breaking into professional work if they had the right qualifications – this was their ticket in, a way of proving they could do the job (women weren't part of an old boys' network which would get them hired by family friends).

That history may have led women to see the workplace as more orderly and meritocratic than it really is: they overestimate the importance of formal training and qualifications, and underutilise advocacy and networking.

Then again, it's possible that women are consciously, or sub-consciously, aware of the biases that act against them, in which case self-selecting out is a wise course of action that saves wasting time and protects their reputation. It's likely that in many organisations women *do* need to meet more of the qualifications to be hired than men. McKinsey's research has persistently found that men are hired or promoted based on their potential, while women are selected for their experience and track record.

If women are more self-protective, and more concerned about potential failure than men, this may also be wise: there is evidence from conformational bias studies, carried out by Raymond Nickerson at Tufts University, that women's failures are remembered longer than men's.

One senior executive with a South American mining company told us she has women come to her to discuss whether they should go for major promotions. Whilst she welcomes the conversations she sometimes finds herself being asked to make the decision *for* the woman. She knows that's because applying for the role and *not* getting it would affect the woman's reputation in the company, so they try to push the difficult decision onto someone else.

3 The response to assertive women

A third explanation for why women are believed not to be confident is that women project self-confidence in a different way and that this is *interpreted* as a lack of confidence.

Giving credit to the team rather than their own efforts, working collaboratively rather than pushing their agenda and allowing others to speak first, can all be interpreted as a lack of confidence. The behaviours which are viewed as confident ("assured", "assertive", "thrusting"...) are masculine behaviours that don't match how women naturally behave. And women who *do* adopt a stereotypically male style of confidence find they are challenging the social hierarchy in ways that are damaging for their careers. (We discuss the backlash effect further in Chapter 14 in this half of the book.)

Attitudes towards women are changing, but there is plenty of research and anecdotal evidence that women can still pay heavy social and professional penalties for acting in a way that is interpreted as aggressive or even assertive.

Women are penalised for being as confident as men

Our female research participants said in the main they still couldn't walk into their boss's office with unsolicited opinions, or be the first to speak up at a meeting, or give a business opinion "above her pay grade", without risking harsh comments like "she's rather full of herself," and "better at talking than listening."

And it won't win her friends. As she progresses higher in the organisation, so will the terms of criticism escalate. A tough male negotiator might be described as "playing hard-ball"; an equally tough woman will likely be called "a bit of a ball-breaker." Note: it's not just her competence or judgement that is criticised: it's her character.

And watch out for the b-word: how quickly is a successful woman referred to as "quite a tough bitch," or "a bit of a pushy bitch." For a man to be referred to as "a bastard" his behaviour needs to be extreme and usually self-serving. But the evidence shows that a woman may be referred to as "a real bitch" for little more than expressing a strong opinion or doing what is right for the organisation.

Women who want to avoid this type of labelling may be consciously or unconsciously adopting a low-confrontation style of behaviour (which looks a lot like a lack of confidence) to avoid being penalised. In which case, no amount of confidence training is going to speed their progression up the ranks.

Holding back, questioning, sharing the credit

In *The Sexual Paradox* Susan Pinker says that women are more inclined to feel they must know everything before speaking, while men are often happy to know 50% and bluff the rest. Women tend to minimise their certainty and men their doubts. This may create the impression that women lack confidence, but it may in fact be a wiser attitude to bring to business decisions.

Women tend to ask more questions: again, a useful habit which broadens the field of focus, and ensures that decisions are made with reference to all the relevant information; but it can be interpreted as uncertainty. Women also tend to be more collaborative, gathering other opinions before making an important decision.

Another potentially misunderstood behaviour is women's tendency to attribute success to the team and failures to themselves. And a study by linguist Deborah Tannen provides evidence that what comes across as lack of confidence on the part of women may reflect a desire not to seem boastful. And recognition of our uncertainty in any situation may spur women, not unreasonably, to do diligent preparation.

One respondent to the Head Heart + Brain research said that what is needed is "Cultural recognition that there are different ways of managing. For example, it can be just as effective to be thoughtful and collaborative. It's not necessary to be aggressive."

But many of the men and women in the research said women need more than belief in themselves. Many women are well qualified and doing good work but most organisations look for more than that: success demands positioning, networks, sponsors (more on those in Chapters 5 and 13 in the other half of the book).

Build your confidence

We need to notice what it is that gets people ahead. Talent isn't just about being competent. Confidence is an important part of what is looked for in talent reviews and promotion criteria. If you don't want to adopt the male style of confidence, and many women don't, make sure you have sponsors and allies who recognise your brand of it. Or, as one of our respondents said, we need to learn to fake it. Success may depend on "being able to paint on a layer of confidence that I do not have," she said: "Blarney, as many men do."

The "believe in yourself" mantra was ideally suited to the nineties and the noughties: truly believe in yourself and all will be right. But a growing body of data suggests that trying to boost your self-esteem without changes in the organisational environment is difficult if not impossible. So, what useful insights can neuroscience offer, and how can they help you manage your inner strengths?

Self-esteem and status

A sense of self-esteem is closely linked to reputation (your social status), and is a vital part of our personal interactions. We hold mental maps of the social hierarchies that are important to us (our families, work groups or regulars at the wine bar) and are acutely aware of everyone's relative position.

The trouble with social ranking is when it's challenged. At some point, we all experience a downward shift. This can happen explicitly: someone doesn't laugh at your joke, your boss disagrees with you publicly, or you don't get the permanent appointment after "acting up" in a role. Or it can be triggered by implicit micro-behaviours: the boss always looks at his phone when you speak in a meeting; a colleague rolls their eye at your suggestion. At these times our low self-esteem "involuntary defeat response" kicks in. We turn tail, and look and feel as though there's no fight left in us.

You know your reaction when you feel defeated: you beat yourself up, undervalue your skills, and feel inclined to steer clear of challenges: "I'll just keep my head down and get on with the job." It's a way of reducing your visibility and avoiding further humiliation, and scientists believe this reduction in activity is a self-protective behaviour that gives us time to regroup.

Hormones that create our self-esteem

Studies with human and non-human primates suggest that changes in the levels of the neurotransmitter serotonin, linked to feelings of wellbeing and happiness, play an important role in regulating self-esteem and our sense of place within the social hierarchy.

Research indicates that high serotonin levels in the brain produce a sense of high self-esteem and social status, while low serotonin levels produce the opposite. High serotonin levels are associated with calm assurance, which leads to smoothly controlled movements. Low serotonin levels are associated with the irritability that leads to impulsive, uncontrolled, reckless and even violent behaviour.

Social feedback creates fluctuations from our baseline serotonin levels, and these fluctuations are part of what determines our current level of self-esteem. Serotonin fluctuations help us to negotiate social hierarchies, to move up as far as circumstances permit, and to be reasonably content at each stage.

This suggests that a high or low level of self-esteem (and serotonin) isn't innate and permanent. Successful people may suffer a fall in social status, self-esteem, and serotonin levels when they have a setback. Equally, success within your social hierarchy elevates your self-esteem and serotonin levels, and each elevation further raises social expectations, perhaps spurring us to try for a promotion or leadership role we wouldn't have previously considered.

The level of serotonin encourages us to strive for more and provides us with a way of coping, helping us to be content to play a group role that's consistent with current limitations.

Boost your confidence hormones

You can "trick" your brain into producing serotonin by reflecting on significant achievements from your past and re-living the experience. Your brain has trouble telling the difference between what's real and imagined, so it produces serotonin in both cases. Imagine yourself feeling confident, being successful at the meeting and smiling at the congratulations from colleagues.

And when the going gets tough, take a few minutes to mentally review your past successes, what you know you are good at and your triumphs. This sounds deceptively simple but it works.

Self-compassion rather than self-esteem

You may find the idea of working to boost your self-esteem doesn't sit well with you. In which case you'll be interested to know that a growing body of research, including studies by Berkeley psychologists Juliana Breines and Serena Chen, suggests that *self-compassion*, rather than self-esteem, may be the key to managing the impact of setbacks and social status changes, and unlocking our full potential.

Self-compassion is a willingness to look at our mistakes and shortcomings with kindness and understanding. It includes accepting that as humans our social status will move both up and down. When we are self-compassionate we neither judge ourselves harshly, nor feel the need to defend and protect ourselves.

And the studies suggest not only does self-compassion *feel* good, it has a positive impact on performance. In their studies, Breines and Chen asked participants to take either a self-compassionate or a self-esteem enhancing view of a setback or failure. For example, when asked to reflect on a personal weakness, some were asked to "Imagine that you are talking to yourself about this weakness from a compassionate and understanding perspective. What would you say?" Others were asked to focus on boosting their self-esteem: "Imagine that you are talking to yourself about this weakness from a perspective of validating your positive qualities. What would you say?"

Compassion improves performance

People in the self-compassion group were more likely to see their weaknesses as changeable: "I know I'm not that great at maths but I can learn and get help to check my calculations." Self-compassion actually *increased* their motivation to improve and avoid the same mistake again in the future.

And this increased motivation led to better performance. For example, in one study participants who failed an initial test were given a second chance to improve their scores. Those who were directed to take a self-compassionate view of their earlier failure studied 25% longer and scored higher in the second test than participants who focused on bolstering their self-esteem.

Self-compassion seems to be powerful because it is not judging. You can confront your flaws and failures, get a realistic sense of your abilities and decide what to do differently next time.

But when your focus is on protecting your self-esteem, you can't afford to look at yourself honestly and acknowledge the need for improvement, because it creates a threat to social status that triggers avoidance, and a tendency to move away from the issue. The key to success is to learn from mistakes and keep moving forward. Self-compassion is a way of approaching mistakes without feeling threatened.

When reflecting on a personal weakness or a performance you are unhappy with use Breines and Chen's approach: "Imagine that you are talking to yourself about this weakness from a compassionate and understanding perspective. What would you say?"

Career hacks

Self-promotion without bragging

One of the behaviours which contribute to the perception that women lack confidence is our different way of talking about our accomplishments. Or, rather, *not* talking about them.

In western culture, stereotyped masculinity is associated with dominating a conversation, being comfortable taking credit and pointing to achievements. (There is evidence that in Asia boys are socialised to be more restrained.) Women, meanwhile, are socialised to be modest, to hide their capabilities or belittle them for fear of boasting.

Eight ways to publicise our skills and achievements that you are comfortable with:

1. Get someone else to blow your trumpet for you. When you're starting a new job, prompt the senior manager who made your appointment to introduce you to the team, and email them the highlights of your CV (and perhaps a couple of personal details). Or if this isn't something they will do, this is a very acceptable time to send that introductory email yourself.
2. As we detail in Chapter 4, find language that you feel comfortable with. Volunteering "I *enjoy* doing presentations / handling supplier negotiations" gives the same message as "I'm good at..." without bragging.
3. A Head Heart + Brain survey respondent told us her tactics include letting her accomplishments emerge during the course of a conversation: "Yes, I was the lead on that deal" or "Yes we have a relationship with organisation X. My role includes leading on their account."
4. Follow Sheryl Sandberg's simple tip of listing prestigious appointments on the shared calendar or as part of your out-of-office notifications. An unvarnished "out of office" auto email response could just be a dentist appointment. A meeting with the sales director of a target company signals your status.
5. Don't forget to keep a record of your key achievements and the numbers attached to them – you'll need them later.
6. And it's no longer the sign of a fantastically successful executive to be too busy to take care of your social media

profile. Keep your LinkedIn profile up to date, as well as any similar internal documentation and your details on the company website.

7. One of the women in the Head Heart + Brain research set up a regular email "newsletter" summary – ostensibly to update her team but also circulated to senior colleagues. She makes sure the team's accomplishments are recognised as well as her own

8. Don't miss an opportunity to share good news (some press coverage, or meeting a critical delivery date...). And when crediting the team use the word "we" ("We achieved the target delivery date for product x"). It sends a sub-conscious message to your boss and other senior people that you were involved; just mentioning the team doesn't.

Group-praise

This is a key point to bear in mind: you can insulate yourself from being labelled as self-promoting if you're consistently generous in promoting group accomplishments.

One important message from the women responding to the Head Heart + Brain research was to share credit generously and help other people along the way – especially as you move up and begin to leave peers behind. Acknowledging how someone had helped you costs nothing and makes lasting allies. One woman told us, "You never know where someone will end up. Keep people close and thank them when they help you, no matter in how small a way."

Louise used to feel angry and disappointed with herself whenever she didn't perform at the top of her game. She's never found the kind of boosterism of "look how great I really am" very convincing, or that it had any lasting effect. She now understands that the kind of confidence she was being expected to express was probably a very male pattern of behaviour.

She and a couple of other women she works with now make a point of mentioning each other's successes, and she's also started circulating a weekly email which highlights her team's achievements – she makes sure it goes to her business unit director, and also to the team's clients as a project update.

Exploring further

Books

The Confidence Code: The Science and Art of Self Assurance, Katty Kay and Claire Shipman

The Sexual Paradox, Susan Pinker

Articles, blogs and podcasts

Women Do Like to Compete – Against Themselves, Coren Apicella and Johanna Mollerstrom. (Creating opportunities for self-competition in the workplace is one way to make women as competitive as men.) New York Times

The Confidence Code: The Science and Art of Self Assurance – What Women Should Know, Katty Kay and Claire Shipman (To become more confident, women need to stop thinking so much and just act.) The Atlantic

Presence: the art of charm, Amy Cuddy (Podcast covering aspects of the social psychologist's influential book.) SoundCloud (51:14)

Videos and webinars

The Imposter Syndrome, Kirsty Walker. TEDx (8:22)

How students of colour confront imposter syndrome, Dena Simmons. (Simmons knows that for students of colour, success in school sometimes comes at the cost of living authentically.) TED.com (10:20)

Always #Like a Girl, Lauren Greenfield (Part of the Always movement to keep girls' confidence high during puberty and beyond, redefining "like a girl" as a positive affirmation.) YouTube (3:19)

The Surprising Secret to Speaking with Confidence, Caroline Goyder (A personal story of moving from stage-paralysis to expressive self, accompanied by an unusual prop.) TEDx (18:56)

How to speak up when you feel like you can't, Adam Galinsky (Research and helpful tips on how to find your voice when it matters most, and to advocate for others who need it.) TEDx (15:03)

What Women Should Know About Self Assurance, CBS This Morning (Interview with author and BBC journalist Katty Kay on how women can improve their confidence to get ahead.) CBS (4:35)

Women in the Google Workplace, Lazlo Bock (The head of HR at Google talks at the Women in the Economy Conference about the behavioral differences between men and women in Google's culture when putting themselves forward for promotion and interview.) Wall Street Journal (4:32)

8.
How performance reviews are stacked against you

Louise and Matt are progressing at Multinational Trading, now both working for the business unit director, although on different teams.

Louise is disappointed, and angry, after her first performance review with her new boss, which was very negative. Previously she's been quite demoralised by any critical assessment, but at least she felt it was fair and she made determined efforts to strengthen the areas she was weak in. She hasn't come away with any direction on specific areas she can improve in. Comparing herself with her peers whose work he seems to favour, she gets the impression that she's never going to be able to please this boss: her style is very different, and he doesn't seem to think the work she's doing is very important.

Matt had a good overall performance evaluation rating but the boss commented on his style. He finds it irritating: like Louise, he thinks their boss is more concerned about style than outcome.

You're on a car journey and stop to ask a couple by the side of the road for directions:

> The man says: "Head north and take the left going east. After just over two miles take the turning on the right going north-east and keep going until the road divides. Go west: it's on the right after about half a mile."

> The woman says: "Head straight down this road until you come to the George and Falcon: take a left there. After quite a way you'll come to a row of five or six shops. Take the right turn in the middle of them. At the top of the steep hill the road divides. Take the left fork by the cottage with a red gate. The place you want is on the right, after the metal fencing. If you reach the school you have gone too far."

These are examples of different male/female styles of explaining directions. When a manager is evaluating performance, if the team members is *like* them the manager is much more likely to understand how they summarise information, present reports and describe their performance. But just as there are different but equally effective ways of working, there can, and should be, recognition that these different styles can be equally valuable, as they foster diversity.

Performance is in the eye of the beholder

Our brains have a natural tendency to sort information into groups to make processing easier, and this can lead us to make snap judgments about people without even realising it.

A study on the way performance ratings are made, by researcher and consultant Marcus Buckingham found that on average 61% of an assessment is based on how the manager thinks the job *should* be done rather than the actual achievements of the person being evaluated.

Managers have a bias for expecting people to carry out work in the same way they would do it, which distorts ratings and can lead to favouritism. The evaluation is more revealing of the manager than the performance of the employee, says Buckingham.

And this doesn't just apply to ratings: research by Paola Cecchi-Dimeglio at the Harvard Law School found that women and men also get radically different feedback. (see next chapter on Feedback) In her findings using content analysis of individual annual performance reviews, she discovered that women were more likely to receive critical subjective feedback ("Louise needs to connect more with clients") than critical objective feedback or any kind of positive feedback.

If managers tend to evaluate people on how they would perform in the role then male managers will be biased towards the work style of male employees. And subjective evaluations open the door to gender-biased statements like "Matt is more confident and independent than Louise in handling clients" and confirmation bias such as "I knew Louise would struggle with the task."

Why are performance reviews so important?

Women remain underrepresented in roles that are the highest in authority, responsibility, and prestige in organisations. And there's no doubt that this is partly attributable to gender stereotypes in the performance appraisal processes.

Yes, prominent women do benefit from some superstar visibility according to the social psychologists Patricia Linville and Edward Jones. Women get polarised evaluations, with exceptional high-flyers getting better evaluations than men, but women who are merely excellent getting lower ratings than comparable men. This is because people, including managers, tend to give higher evaluations to exceptional people in the out-group whereas evaluations of their in-group are more nuanced (they notice some strengths and weaknesses.)

Merely-excellent women's lower ratings accumulate and impede their progress up the hierarchy. This has been graphically demonstrated by a computer simulation constructed by programmers at Northwestern University inspired by Alice Eagly's seminal work *Through the Labyrinth: The Truth About How Women Become Leaders.*

The model of a fictional company had 500 employees at the bottom and 10 at the top. At the start the gender balance was equal at both levels. Each employee was assigned an evaluation rating and promoted accordingly, with employees with the highest ratings moving up. The simulation gave male employees 1% higher ratings on average to represent the real-life effects of gender bias. After a short time the number of women at the top level had dropped to only a third while 53% of the bottom positions were held by women. And this type of simulation doesn't reflect the additional effect that the increasing imbalance has in depressing women's expectations and aspirations.

What *should* evaluations be measuring?

We are all naturally suspicious of the effect of informal, old-boy networks, and mates giving friends a leg up, in maintaining men's dominance of corporate management. It's not good enough anymore for a group of directors just to sit around a table and pick their (male) successors. We tend to have more confidence in ostensibly objective tools such as performance evaluations, which many fine minds in business management have spent thousands of hours refining.

But several embarrassed Human Resources Directors (they were the honest ones) regretfully told Head Heart + Brain that they were aware that performance evaluations were harsher for women than for men. Given that annual assessments are the well-established method for deciding salary, bonuses and promotion, and are the gateway to mentors, development training and fast-track talent programmes, this is a damning indictment of a process that may well be one of the structural supports of the iniquitous glass ceiling.

Getting evaluated for your contribution to a team

When women are working in teams (as is increasingly the case in modern organisations), there's often ambiguity about who contributed what. Research has found that when women work in groups with men and no information is given to their manager about individual contributions, women's contributions are routinely devalued.

In three experiments by Aparna Joshi at Penn State, participants were given information either about the group or about individual performance of specific tasks relating to a group outcome. When the only information available was about the group's performance, women were rated as less competent, having less influence, and taking less of a leadership role than their male counterparts.

But when participants had clear information about specific and unique tasks that the women employees completed, the differences in perceptions between the genders disappeared.

Likewise, if the assessors in the experiment were given unequivocally positive information about the women's effective performances in *previous* work, women's contributions were sometimes rated higher than the men's, even when only group performance information was available to the assessors. This suggests assessors are influenced by the "halo effect" of previous performance.

One of our research participants, a senior leader in HR, told us it's difficult for women when they move from one manager to another: the organisation's systems rarely keep good details of past achievements. What this means is that women need to be sure to record their contribution to a team project (or any work), and make sure their manager has that information, and that they have a record for any future managers, to reduce any ambiguity. Tilt the balance in your favour by priming their expectations with details of your positive performance in previous tasks. (More on specific feedback tools which can facilitate this in the following chapter.)

The assessment of potential

One of the developments in appraisal and talent processes in organisations has been to assess for potential as well as actual performance. These systems look at the skills and experience of people in the organisation and try to predict the level they can reach. Whilst organisations create criteria, usually in the form of leadership frameworks, the assessment of potential is often subjective. A team of leaders, such as the management or talent committee will look at past performance and the leadership criteria and make a judgement about potential to rise in the hierarchy.

Women now occupy 50% of middle management positions, but less than a third of positions in upper management.

Financial skills development: neglected for women

For the highest roles, most companies have criteria which include business, strategic, and financial acumen – or the ability to understand the financial side of the business. Susan Colantuono, CEO and founder of the Leading Women consultancy, says this is the skill that is missing in the advice given to women – not because they are incapable of achieving it, but because it isn't a skill they are advised to acquire.

The assumption that women focus on relationships, teamwork and collaboration subtly excludes them from gaining experience in parts of the business where financial and strategic skills would be acquired. And this lack of experience often stems from the advice women are given right from the start of their careers. One female survey respondent told us: "My careers officer at university suggested three careers for me based on my degree (French & Italian): bilingual secretary, teacher or marry a rich man. A male friend on the same degree course was recommended to consider international banking." (The woman now works in professional services.)

Colantuono asks women how many have been told that financial and strategic skills are important, and finds that very few have been given this critical advice. Women are encouraged to develop negotiating skills, personal branding, networking and self-confidence, which are good advice for reaching middle management positions, but will not be enough to reach executive level. In addition, many performance and talent development programmes focus on personal achievement and leadership, and are not filling in the gaps in financial and strategic skills.

Evaluating women as future leaders

Women need to get assignments which build experience in these areas in order to improve their chances of making it up into the ranks of leadership. But Catalyst, the think tank promoting organisational change in diversity, has found that men's potential to lead (and, in particular, their potential to lead effectively), is rarely questioned prior to an appointment. Women, by contrast, typically must prove that they can fulfil the role before they gain promotion.

Catalyst's research paper *The Promise of Future Leadership: Highly Talented Employees in the Pipeline* shows how women are consistently evaluated more negatively on factors such as performance, leadership ability and problem-solving. And women evaluators can demonstrate this bias too. The research showed that male managers doing evaluations tend to express more doubts about female leaders' effectiveness than women do. But both men and women are more positive about men in supervisory roles than women.

In general, women are more likely to receive positive evaluations when they occupy leadership roles defined in feminine terms (requiring supporting and mentoring skills), but negative evaluations on masculine measures of leadership – problem-solving and being assertive.

The answer is not to give more weight to potential for growth than look for proven skills and experience which women may not have. Harvard professor of public policy, Iris Bohnet, has found that organisations that use potential, in addition to performance, to evaluate employees are *more* likely to also be gender-biased. This is hardly surprising, she says, because potential is often vaguely defined and more difficult to measure than performance. In our own research we were unable to find a single organisation that had scrutinised their leadership framework and criteria for bias towards masculine traits. (See Chapter 15 in this half of the book on Leadership.)

Our own worst enemies? Women underrate their own performance

A study by Scott Taylor at the University of New Mexico Anderson School of Management showed that female managers are more than three times as likely as men to underrate their bosses' opinions of their job performance. And this discrepancy increases with women over 50. "Women have imposed their own glass ceiling," say the researchers, "and the question is why."

In the study the men slightly overestimated how their bosses would rate them. And the women managers underestimated their ratings on average by about 11%. Interestingly, there was also a generational difference: "Younger women tended not to be as off-base in their predictions as middle-aged or senior women," Taylor comments. He thinks it could be that older women under rate themselves due to the negative value placed on age in the workplace.

And we agree that's the case. A 54 year-old woman in our survey illustrates Taylor's findings: "I thought the most difficult time for me as a working woman would be when I had children. It wasn't. The most difficult time was when I became older and gender plus age meant I was no longer considered to have the time to realise potential in the way younger colleagues were. Every time I have been for promotion since hitting 48 (five times now) I have been pipped at the post by someone young and male; I was told it was close and they thought I could do the job, but they made a decision based on potential not experience."

Taylor concludes that managers need to learn better ways to communicate to female employees that they are valued. And women need to get better at seeking positive as well as critical feedback for themselves.

The pitfalls of self-evaluation

When self-evaluation was introduced into performance assessment in the early 2000s, It might have been hoped that trying to incorporate the views of the employee would give women employees an opportunity to frame success in their own terms.

But Iris Bohnet has shown self-evaluations can be a double-edged sword, because women self-assess lower than men. And managers of mixed teams who see their employees' self-assessments before they have completed their own grading of their staff are influenced by the self-ratings. This tends to work against women: "I thought she was doing well but she doesn't seem to think so, maybe I should shave that rating back a bit."

Behavioural science shows that we are anchored by the numbers we first see, so Bohnet recommends not sharing employee self-evaluations with managers before they have made and recorded their own judgements.

Joint evaluations for promotion give women a better chance

When promotion decisions are made for senior positions, they are usually done one at a time (by a line manager), or in meetings with several managers where performance or potential is calibrated against other people up for promotion. These individual processes are vulnerable to the implicit gender biases that are automatically activated when evaluators know a candidate's gender. Another study by Iris Bohnet at Harvard has looked at how joint evaluations by more than one evaluator can make hiring, job assignment, performance evaluations and promotion processes more impartial.

The Harvard study found that in separate evaluations men were usually chosen over equally qualified women for male-stereotypical jobs or projects. And lower-performing men were even chosen over higher-performing women. Employers preferred women to equally qualified men for female-stereotypical assignments (marketing, HR or "caring" roles).

But in joint evaluations when a small group consider the applications of all candidates at one time, the gender gap disappeared: employers preferred higher-performing employees to lower-performing employees irrespective of gender, and were as likely to choose women as men.

Employers may make different decisions in joint evaluations because they have directly comparable candidates, and this nudge directs them to take a more information-based approach, relying on performance data rather than implicit, stereotyped judgments. And joint evaluations usually include more information on candidates' abilities such as historical ratings and experience, potentially providing more counter-stereotypical data points and encouraging evaluators to update their beliefs about women's abilities.

Future change

Sadly, Louise will be battling her way up the corporate ladder within an established evaluation and promotion system at Multinational Trading. Hopefully when she makes it to executive level she'll be in a position to push for changes that will help to eliminate corporate bias, but in the meantime some well-worded summaries of the latest research in gendered evaluations, given to key managers and influencers, may help to set some change in motion – and demonstrate her own bigger-picture view.

Career hacks

How to respond to a biased evaluation

When we get a negative evaluation, our brains go into a threat state and will be less resourceful, less creative and less open to new ideas. One of the Head Heart + Brain survey participants said it would be very helpful to have "scripts on how to respond to gender-biased language used in performance feedback."

- If you suspect your manager will give you a poor evaluation which you don't deserve, rehearse what you are going to say and your manager's potential responses.
- To be at your most agile and resourceful, recall a time when you felt on top form and in control.
- Practise saying your questions out loud. For example:

  o "How is my performance evaluated, what criteria were used?"
  o "How does my performance compare to my colleagues, both male and female?"
  o "What's the most *important* criteria in evaluating my performance? Is it the outcome I got? Or is it the route I took to achieve the outcome?"
  o "Can you give me an example of what I would need to do to get the same opportunity as Pete?"
  o "Can you give some specific areas where my performance is less effective than Nick's?"
  o "Who is a role model I can emulate to help me satisfy the criteria?"

Matt has already decided to move away from this boss and he tells Louise she should do the same. Matt has a formal mentor within Multinational Trading and he's asked for help finding other vacancies at his level. He wants to work for someone who's focused on outcomes, not style.

Louise is doing what she can to identify her boss's priorities and tailor her role to meet his expectations. She's also raising her profile with their boss's peers, and focusing on her relationships with clients so their boss hears more positive comments on her via informal channels. She knows her best protection is to have other people telling him how great she is: he won't want to upset a strong client relationship no matter how much he dislikes her approach.

Exploring further

Articles, blogs and podcasts

The Abrasive Trap: High Achieving-Men and Women are Described Differently in Reviews, Kieran Snyder (Research by linguist and recruitment software tech CEO demonstrating the differences in how men and women are described in performance reviews.) Fortune Magazine

Videos

Even After Criticism, Men Think Highly of Themselves, Margarita Mayo (Women are quicker than men to adjust their self-image in line with peer review.) Harvard Business Review Video (1:27)

9.
The feedback trap

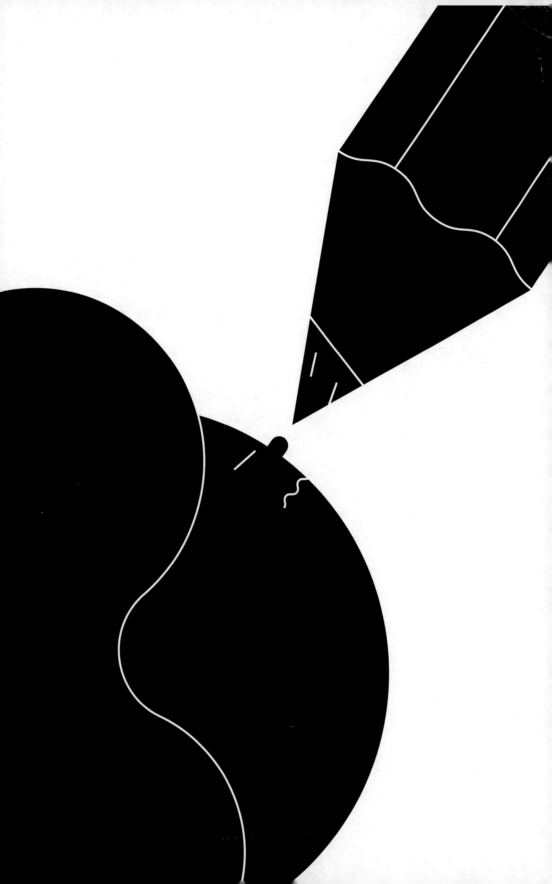

Louise is very disheartened by her first formal feedback from her new boss. She was shocked to be told that she's "somewhat unfocused," "doesn't attend to the priorities," and "goes off and does her own thing."

She doesn't really know what that means; she regularly asks her peers for feedback and they say she's good to work with and is very effective. She's not sure what to do about this feedback – she thinks it's because she doesn't work the same way as her director does.

Matt had some feedback about not being assertive enough with suppliers and clients: he's worked hard on building good relationships that he believes help him get the best results without resorting to threats and bullying. Both he and Louise feel the boss wants them to be just like him and will comment negatively on any style that is different from his.

Feedback is the backbone of many management tools including having a crucial role in performance management and evaluations, training and the potential of development. But how well does feedback serve employees generally and women in particular?

Feedback can be problematic whatever our gender. The most comprehensive review of studies on performance feedback was carried out by Denisi and Kluger and dates back to 1996. They found mixed evidence on the value of feedback and say that about one third of the time feedback leads to improved performance, one third of the time it does nothing, and in a around 40% of examples it leads to worse performance. But the devil is in the details so lets explore a little more.

On simple tasks where people don't have experience feedback can improve performance, in some specific circumstances where there are clear goals. Think about learning to use a new computer programme and someone who is expert tells you how to maximise the use of the tool bar. Feedback can also improve performance on complex tasks in certain conditions when the goal is important to the employee, they think this is because employees are focused on learning and goal attainment and therefore worry less about protecting their reputation as competent.

Denisi and Kluger found that feedback can be *harmful* when given on complex, difficult or unfamiliar tasks. This is because the feedback shifts focus from the task to protecting their self-image and creates a fear of looking incompetent. This negatively impacts performance. Feedback about attitudes and personal traits does not work and damages performance. Based on this it's not really surprising that Louise is unhappy.

Neuroscience evidence on feedback

Neuroscience research has found that just saying 'let me give you some feedback' creates a threat response in the brain. We have discussed threat and reward responses before in Brain Basics in the other end of the book. Feedback can generate threat in each of the CORE elements, unless it is positive feedback. For example, negative feedback impacts the sense of reputation which leads to reduced connection with the group and potentially creates a sense of shame. Negative feedback also impacts certainty; because employees no longer know what is the right work method and it impacts options because being told they are not carrying out the role in the way expected limits their autonomy. Both of which probably feel unfair.

So feedback can be problematic even before we add in the research on gender.

The negative bias for women

Research at Stanford University's Clayman Institute for Gender Research has been examining the effectiveness of feedback used by organisations to redirect behaviour and performance. The work by Shelley Correll and Caroline Simard reveals dramatic differences in the type of feedback received by men and women, and is shedding light on one of the barriers to advancement caused by how gender stereotypes impact feedback.

Correll and Simard found that nearly 88% of the reviews received by women contained critical feedback, compared with just 59% of the reviews received by men.

And the critical constructive feedback men receive is heavily geared towards suggestions for developing additional skills. For example, "Hone your strategies for guiding your team and developing their skills. It is important to set proper guidance around priorities and to help as needed in design and product decisions."

Compare this with the kinds of constructive feedback that women receive, which include a sharper element, "You can come across as abrasive sometimes. I know you don't mean to, but you need to pay attention to your tone."

This kind of negative criticism pointing out things like, watch your tone, step back, stop being so judgmental, showed up twice as much for women than in the critical reviews received by men.

Men's feedback points to growth potential

Feedback for women is expressed in more general terms than for men, the Clayman Institute researchers found. For example, a man might be described in his evaluation as "achieving goals," while a woman colleague "gets things done".

In reviewing decision-making and time management, a similar behaviour may be seen as problematic in a woman ("Louise seems to freeze when facing tight deadlines to make decisions") but as careful thoughtfulness in a man ("Matt seems hesitant in making decisions, yet he is able to work out multiple alternative solutions and consider them thoughtfully").

Most importantly, feedback for a man is often framed in terms of needing to further develop skills he's assumed to already have. The criticism of him is wrapped up in an assumed talent: "Matt needs to develop his natural people skills." There often isn't the same recognition of growth potential when a similar criticism is made of a woman: "Louise lacks self-confidence: she seems to make herself small when she's around the client."

These differences in nuance should not be ignored, say Correll and Simard, because "language is powerful at shaping perceptions."

"Halo" and "horns" feedback

These unthinking biases are not only a significant barrier to women's progression but can be problematic for organisations when men's talents are being overrated due to the "halo effect": where one positive trait is assumed to be linked to others.

Whilst in theory the halo effect is well understood as a bias - one good result is assumed to generalise to others, "Matt won an important piece of business with this client he will do well with others" it is still prevalent especially when there are no checks and balances to raise awareness of its impact. Because the human brain likes certainty, is lazy, preferring to go along with its first impression. And because the brain also tends to have a preference for people categorised as "like me" (see chapter 7 in the other end of the book) leaders can stay committed to an up-and-coming man who was assumed to have the people skills, say, to match his technical expertise, giving him coaching and support long after it has become apparent that he has been over-promoted.

And the reverse can happen to women with the "horns effect" one negative issue – shouting at a team member, getting emotional over the loss of a client – can be generalised to be an established trait or lack of skill. Of course some women get the halo effect and some men get the horns effect, but the research would suggest the bias more often goes the other way.

"Too bossy," "too emotional"...

Analysing performance evaluations for junior male and female attorneys at a Wall Street firm, Madeline Heilman from New York University found that ratings dropped for women who didn't display "interpersonal warmth." "They're out of line, breaking the rules, violating the 'shoulds' of gender stereotypes," says Heilman. "The issue is not: are they that way or not that way. The issue is: men and women are probably behaving exactly the same but women are taking a hit."

Delving further she found that women were more likely to receive feedback that contrasted strongly with the feedback received by men. For example, men might be described as "confident" or "assertive", but the same behaviour in women was considered negative. Common words used in critical reviews of female employees included: *abrasive, bossy, aggressive, strident, emotional* and *irrational*. Of all of these words only the term "aggressive" was used occasionally for men.

And research by Kieran Snyder from the University of Pennsylvania found managers are nearly seven times more likely to tell their male employees that their communication style is too soft. Women, on the other hand, receive more feedback related to being too aggressive.

The Clayman Institute research reveals that the language used for both genders in feedback conforms to stereotypical views of men and women. Not only were women given negative feedback for what was perceived as an aggressive communication style, they were also found to be "supportive", "collaborative" and "helpful" more often than men. The language used to describe men was linked more to confidence and independence, and they were twice as likely to receive feedback based on their technical expertise.

Snyder's research, focusing on the technology industry, found similar results. In performance reviews for women and men she found that women were significantly more likely to receive critical feedback as well as stereotyped feedback.

Teamwork feedback overlooks individual achievement

Women's performance reviews have more than twice as many references to team accomplishments as individual results, and contain nearly twice as much language about their communal or nurturing style, using terms such as "helpful" or "dedicated."

The stereotype is that women are less comfortable claiming credit, and more comfortable attributing an achievement to team effort and other external factors. And managers hold stereotyped views about women being "supportive," "collaborative" and "helpful." But women's individual contributions may be overlooked in applauding team achievements. And this is critically important because many competency frameworks look for attributes such as independence, and promotions research shows there is a strong preference for people rated highly on individual initiative.

We also know that companies look for business contribution, and men are three times more likely to hear feedback related to business outcomes. Men also hear nearly twice as many references to their technical expertise and their vision. Women receive one-third less feedback about business outcomes, and their reviews have half as many words about their technical expertise and having "vision."

Not recognising women's achievements in relation to the bottom-line profitability of the business, nor giving them feedback that they need to build their skills and experience in these areas, does them a great disservice. Later in their careers women will find that a lack of experience in roles with P&L (profit and loss) accountability will be a significant barrier to breaking through to the highest levels of the leadership. Research in the UK by the Pipeline consultancy found only 6% of women on executive committees have P&L responsibility and the number is dropping not increasing.

The future: automated feedback

Paola Cecchi-Dimeglio, senior research fellow at Harvard Law School, has studied the use of tailor-made, automated, verifiable real-time communication tools in professional services firms which enable instant feedback on performance from supervisors, colleagues, and clients. Her results indicate that they can have beneficial results for women.

These systems mean people tend to receive, and give, feedback from and to a wider group of people: those in the team but also those working on connected projects. And women especially are more likely to give feedback and also to give it to people both senior to them and more junior according to research by Pay Compliment a software provider of feedback systems.

These more-frequent feedback opportunities allow for recognition of the different styles of leadership of men and women identified by organisational psychologist Alice Eagly at Northwestern University. She and subsequent researchers have shown that women's leadership styles are less hierarchical and more cooperative, inclusive, and collaborative than the typical male leadership style, and are more easily recognised in feedback coming from multiple sources.

More useful for employees, and managers

All employees gain as they can be evaluated for their actual performance and work relationships, rather than by their boss's impressions, reducing the likelihood of personality-based criticism. And because real-time reviews give examples of effective (or ineffective) behaviour, it encourages self-management: people can see what they should do more or less of.

These systems are extremely useful for managers as well. They get details they have never had before: how consistent employees' performance is, how they grow over the course of a year (or a project cycle), how they respond to feedback over time, their weaknesses and strengths, and how various people attach different weight to the same aspects of performance. Managers learn the kind of support and exposure they need to give each employee to help them maximise their performance.

The best software also provides a diagram of the employee's network of feedback-givers and to whom they give feedback, which demonstrates who has influence in a team, who is supportive of others and who is in touch with work across a whole business unit.

And it's portable

Many of these feedback systems have the added advantage that the employee can take the content with them when moving from one part of an organisation to another, or from one employer to another – providing a history of their achievements.

This may seem insignificant, but large government departments have told us this is a real positive for women, especially those returning from maternity leave. Often they're starting afresh with a new manager or in a new department where their track record isn't known and there's no readily-available, reliable history of their accomplishments.

Not all companies provide this depth and sophistication of feedback and until they do women are wise to keep (and share) clear records and examples of the work they have done.

Career hacks

Dealing with unfair feedback

If you're in your review meeting and the feedback takes you by surprise, now is not the time to have a difficult discussion challenging it. Take these steps:

> • Give yourself time to process your emotions and prepare a considered response by saying something like: "That's extremely disappointing, and not what I was expecting. I'd like some time to consider it properly: can we schedule a meeting when we can discuss it further."
> • Proactively identify the areas of your work that you have not received feedback on, which you believe you perform well in (it may be useful to ask a colleague and ally to reflect on this with you), and ask for formal consideration of the areas to be included.
> • In response to feedback that appears to be gender-stereotyped, ask for clarification in the most open-ended way possible: "Could you describe the behaviour you're looking for in neutral terms?" "Could you clarify for me how 'being pushy' is different from 'being results-driven'?"

Matt and Louise were wary of complaining to HR about the specific feedback they received. But they've researched the latest feedback apps and software systems on the market, and have found an example of best-practice in their industry.

They've made a joint approach to HR about using a more objective feedback tool. They've discovered it's helpful for HR to have support from people within the organisation and that there's good visibility in working on company-wide projects like this.

Exploring further

Books

Through the Labyrinth: The Truth About How Women Become Leaders, Alice Eagly and Linda Carli

Articles, blogs and podcasts

The Gender Gap in Feedback and Self-Perception, Margarita Mayo, Harvard Business Review

Agile Performance, Management blog. Pay Compliment.

Video and webinars

Performance feedback data mining, Pay compliment and Head Heart + Brain webinar. (Webinar on feedback analytics) at Pay compliment blog (50:04)

10.
Presence, and the art of storytelling

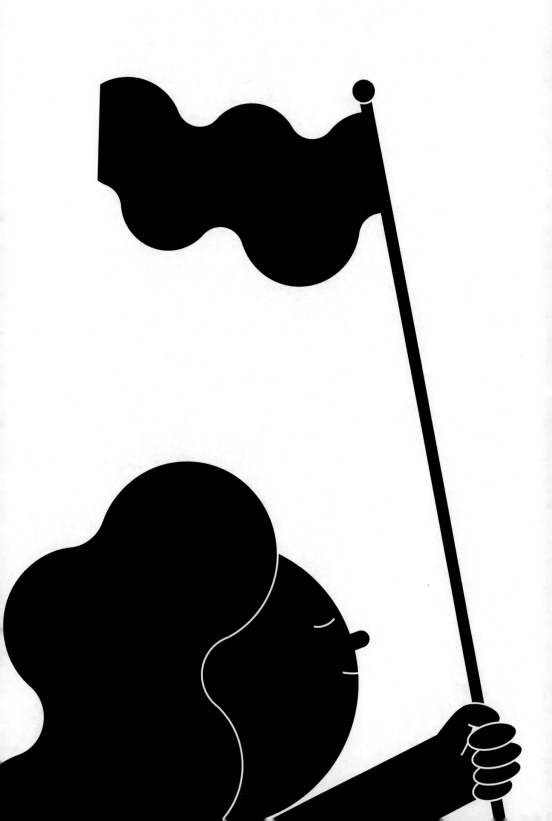

Louise has a new boss who's much more focused on outcomes, and also a mentor (through the organisation's formal talent development programme).

Her mentor is getting her focussed on leadership roles, and has said it would help her if she had more of the x-factor quality of "presence." As far as she understands it, that means commanding attention when she meets potential clients, and being more engaging when she's making presentations.

Louise is a little disheartened: it feels like a quality you either have or you don't. She can't turn herself into a 6ft man with a big voice – and she doesn't want to, either.

One of the issues women told us they consistently received feedback on was what might broadly be described as presence, or their perceived lack of it. "I'm told I need to make more of an impression when I present to clients." "My manager says I need to be more memorable. He spoke to a client I had met who couldn't recall being introduced to me. I mean really: maybe the client had just met lots of people that day!"

What is presence?

Presence is a tricky concept. Conventionally it's related to confidence and a kind of impressive manner that commands attention. People with presence are persuasive with clients and inspiring to employees. The stereotype is easy to picture: a man, probably tall, probably good-looking, who draws the eye when he enters a conference room. (The handsomeness is not coincidental: a 2013 study by Alison Brooks of Harvard Business School demonstrated that investors preferred entrepreneurial pitches made by physically attractive men.)

To aspire to, or be expected to develop this very male definition of "presence" is not a reasonable expectation for women. We're on a hiding to nowhere. But the authors of this book believe there is a more fundamental type of true presence that bypasses stereotypes and is highly accessible to women (as well as to short, less-attractive men).

A new definition of presence

You will have experienced it yourself: that feeling you can get from someone who establishes a sense of connection with you that is almost palpable. It could be expressed by a charismatic leader, a close friend, a nurse or a taxi driver, but for that period of time they are completely focused on you and your needs.

They are *present*, and their ability to be present with you invites you to be present as well: it draws you into more meaningful communication. You can identify these people across the room at after-conference cocktail parties. They're not the ones regaling a group with war-stories of business success. They're the ones who are listening closely, who are engaged in thoughtful conversations that look more like a real exchange of views than performances.

This kind of presence shouldn't be confused with power and status. There are glamorous people who will turn heads as they come into the room, but they may not have this capacity for personal connection – they could always seem rather aloof or more interested in their story rather than the story of the other person. It's possible that their fame and status makes it *harder* for them to connect.

"I see you"

The type of connection we're talking about is summed up in the traditional style of greeting among the tribespeople of northern Natal, in South Africa: "Sawa bona" means literally "I see you." To which the response is *"Sikhona,"* "I am here." It's an exchange that suggests that until you're "seen" you don't exist, and when you are seen you're brought into existence. This is the skill of deeply connecting to other people and giving them attention, and many believe it speaks to a basic human need to be validated.

For many of us this power of being-present is the X-factor in business. It's an invaluable skill for anyone, but especially for women. Everyone is capable of this level of connection. When we achieve it we understand more of what's going on in the business, we're more influential and less likely to be plagued with unhelpful feedback based on stereotypical expectations.

Presence is a feeling state and one of its characteristics is that the experience feels spontaneous to both of the people involved in the conversation. There's no power play, posturing or self-consciousness, and past experience is not interfering with the interaction. There's also an element of energy.

The power of "honest signals"

Psychology has for many years emphasised the importance of not just words in communication, but also the power of body language and tone of voice. People watch and make judgements on what is real and relevant to them, and what is for show. This is largely intuitive, but research from Sandy Pentland at MIT has been able to verify and even put numbers on these factors. (We've referred to this research in Chapter 10 on teamwork in the other half of the book.)

Pentland found that we act on and are influenced by the "honest signals" people send – the unconscious and non-verbal language that includes tone and energy. These signals contrast with "dishonest" signals that may be employed, for example, when someone is pretending to be interested.

Learning to be a "charismatic connector"

Pentland says that the ability to communicate "honest signals" is a significant factor in the success of individuals and teams, and can gain bigger pay rises and win business pitches. As he points out, we all recognise this at some level. We know when a leader or a team is being effective and productive and can notice the difference when they are not. Pentland has found that a particular type of person is most effective in teams; he calls them "charismatic connectors" and they have many of the characteristics we associate with presence. They mainly work to connect people and information, talking to everybody and driving conversation around the team.

Pentland found that people can be trained to amplify their honest signals by putting in more energy, and to communicate more effectively by using non-verbal cues. His research indicates that when people are communicating honestly there is better understanding and increased motivation and productivity in a team.

What inhibits our ability to be present?

If the ability to connect is a learnable skill why aren't we all charismatically connected? In discussions with clients at Head Heart + Brain we find these are the main issues:

> **Distractions:** everything from automatically checking our phones to having a discussion standing by a desk distracted by other conversations rather than walking to a meeting area.
> **Internal dialogue:** all that noise in our heads, which might be self-consciousness, planning what to say next, or wondering what the other person thinks of us.
> **Threat response:** we may start by being closely engaged but lose it when we feel "threatened" by what the person is saying, or how they're saying it. We need to be comfortable to stay present. (The CORE model which we describe in Brain Basics in Chapter 1 of the other half of the book can help you identify what's triggering your disconnection.)
> **Judgement:** we make judgements all the time. Is this person being honest? Have they said what they really feel? Judgements block our ability to listen, close down curiosity and reduce empathy. We need to catch ourselves doing it, and make a conscious effort to suspend judgement.
> **Habit:** we can just get into the habit of not fully connecting and not paying attention to the other person and instead do any of the things listed above.

Learning the skills

Research suggests we can learn these skills and even fake them until we get really good at them. Harvard social psychologist Amy Cuddy has shown that when people adopt new postures, such as appearing more powerful, or appearing more confident in what we are saying, the brain starts to change and the adopted approach can be integrated into everyday behaviour.

In other research Helen Riess, director of the Empathy and Relational Science Program at Boston's Massachusetts General Hospital, has been teaching doctors to be empathetic with patients by monitoring themselves. Her programme taught participants to focus using deep, diaphragmatic breathing and to cultivate a detachment – to watch an interaction from the ceiling, as it were, rather than being lost in their own thoughts and feelings. "Suspending your own involvement to observe what's going on gives you a mindful awareness of the interaction without being completely reactive," says Riess. "You can see if your own physiology is charged up or balanced. You can notice what's transpiring in the situation."

Presence requires practice

The *experience* of presence may feel spontaneous and unpractised, but if you've got out of the habit of connecting with people in this way, or you have never learnt the skills, you will need to apply some conscious effort to exercise the art of being present:

> **Develop personal awareness:** being present for others depends on your mood at any given time, and being able to change it. Practise noticing your state and naming it, and be aware of "What do I do, how do I do it, and why do I do it."
> **Develop physical awareness:** you speak through your body, and as Pentland's research has shown, people pick up on this and respond to it. Everyone needs the quotation from Ralph Waldo Emerson somewhere close at hand: "Who you are speaks so loudly I can't hear what you are saying." Until these skills become second nature, don't go into an interaction without re-tuning for the right degree of energy and confidence.
> **Exercise emotional control:** you need to be able to step outside the immediate interaction, sense what is working and what is not, and make the required adjustments.

Being curious is a great help: it's nearly impossible to be judgemental or listen to your own internal dialogue if you are deeply curious about the other person.

Presence calls for practice and intention, which means believing it's a worthwhile skill to acquire, and comparing how it feels when you are present with someone to when you're distracted. Noticing the difference in your influence will help you to practise "seeing" other people.

People with presence are great story-tellers

One way that people achieve presence is through the way they tell stories. Stories told to our emotional and rational brains are heard by our conscious and unconscious minds. Consider the following tale and observe your emotional responses:

A powerful businessman found a brightly coloured caterpillar on the plant decorating his office; it was beginning to spin its cocoon. He observed it over the following weeks until one day he noticed a small split had appeared in the cocoon. The butterfly was going to emerge!

The businessman was fascinated. He showed the struggling insect inside its cocoon to everyone who came to his office for a meeting that afternoon. This was a lesson worth learning: the imagination of a little grub to turn into a beautiful butterfly.

But after a few hours he became concerned. The butterfly wasn't managing to break free. Perhaps some butterflies never managed to escape their cocoons? The businessman called for his secretary who ran to bring him the sharpest scissors. He carefully snipped the cocoon and the butterfly quickly emerged.

The man was shocked to see that it had a swollen body and small, shrivelled wings. He continued to watch, thinking the wings would unfurl and expand and the butterfly would become the jewelled creature he was waiting for. He would open his office window and let it fly away across the skyscrapers of the city.

But the swollen body didn't shrink; the crumpled wings didn't grow. The butterfly spent the rest of its short life crawling around unable to fly.

The man ordered his secretary to find a butterfly expert who told him what had gone wrong(she just googled it.) The butterfly's struggle to push its way through the tiny opening in the cocoon would squeeze the fluid out of its body and into its expanding wings. Without the struggle, the butterfly would never, ever have the wings that would enable it to fly.

Every culture uses stories to pass on knowledge and wisdom and many organisations are adopting the same approach to communicate their messages and values. Stories are powerful tools for influencing, and once you know how our brains respond to stories, it's easy to understand why.

What happens when we listen

Neuroscience has identified that our brains react to stories in very different ways to receiving information from a PowerPoint presentation, for instance. When we're sitting looking at the words and bullet-points up on a screen, the language-processing areas of our brains (Broca's area and Wernicke's area) are activated to decode their meaning.

When we're listening to a story these same areas are activated, but also the areas of our brains that process visual images, or the emotions.

Brain synchronisation

And when people tell stories which are intended to shape thinking and pass on wisdom, the brains of their listeners synchronise with the storyteller's. Work by psychologist Uri Hasson at Princeton has found that similar brain regions are activated in both listener and the storyteller, including the insula which provides emotional context and integrates information, and the frontal cortex which is responsible for analytical and control functions.

Even more remarkably, the study also identified a subset of brain regions in which the responses in the listener's brain *preceded* the prompts in the speaker's brain. These anticipatory responses suggest that listeners actively predict a storyteller's words. The Princeton research found that the more extensive the join-up between a speaker's brain response and a listener's anticipatory brain response, the better the listener understood the story. Our brains have developed a common neural protocol that allows us to use such brain coupling to share information effectively.

And a Canadian meta-analysis of 86 studies has shown there's substantial overlap in the brain networks we use to understand stories and the networks we use to understand other people – especially when we're trying to understand other people's thoughts and feelings.

Since the regions activated are associated with the ability to simulate the minds of other people, it appears that to be an effective influencer you need to be thinking, when you first hear some information, about how you can communicate it to others in a useful and interesting way.

Telling a story to be re-told

How does this affect Louise, who wants to get her director to propose her new idea to the CEO and the rest of the board?

UCLA's Matt Lieberman and his colleague Emily Falk have studied what happens in the brain when people hear an idea that they know they will want to pass on to someone else, and which they will relay in such a way that the second person will also pass it on.

Before this study, it was assumed that when people are exposed to new information – a new story – they're assessing whether the information is sufficiently useful for them to pay close attention to it, and try to remember it. Lieberman's experiments showed that actually we are just as focused on social concerns: we're assessing whether the information is of value to other people who are important to us, and not just whether it's important to ourselves. And when we know we're going to want to pass on this story the brain regions associated with understanding other people are active rather than just the memory systems of the brain.

Being an information DJ

Lieberman calls this being an information DJ – people think about who else the information will be useful to, and have other people's interests in mind when they first encounter it. And the more important they feel it is to others, the better able they are to pass on the information in a way that also resonates with others. It seems that as people hear or read the information they are simultaneously working out how to pass it on so that it is interesting and meaningful to the next person.

Lieberman suggests that the brain's reward systems are activated because telling an effective story increases the storyteller's sense of reputation within their group. So Louise needs to consider how her proposal is going to appeal to her immediate boss, before she thinks about how the CEO will receive it.

She needs to hook him in with a story about the kind of problem that it's going to solve, or the inspiring work that's been done to come up with this radical solution. She can prime him to listen as though he's going to pass on the story by saying something like "This seems to be the kind of solution the CEO's looking for when he told us…"

Using stories to communicate effectively

Neuroscientist and psychologist Mary Helen Immordino-Yang has found that when we hear inspirational stories more blood flows to the brain stem – that part of our brain which makes our heart beat, regulates our breathing and keeps us alive. It seems that we experience a story's inspirational message at the very core of our biological survival mechanism.

These findings have important implications for passing on your ideas, being influential and thinking about how you tell your story. It suggests that all of this depends more on your social-cognitive abilities, use of emotions, and motivation, and less on IQ-type intelligence. None of the brain regions involved in storytelling make use of the brain regions associated with higher-level abstract reasoning and executive functioning.

So, the next time you want to be truly present and connect with your boss or your client, make sure you're putting yourself in their shoes, and you're thinking about what they want to know, and pass on. And if you're struggling to get people on board with your projects or ideas, tell them a story which has the same ending you're trying to achieve: it's a powerful way to plant ideas into other people's minds.

Career hacks

How to tell a story

If you need to make a presentation, plan it as a story. If you think about your favourite films / urban stories / fairy tales / popular songs (the music, not the lyrics) you'll see a common pattern of descent and return, diving and emerging.

This technique, adapted from Joseph Campbell's work on Myth and Heroes will help you to craft a story. Start by drawing a circle and dividing it into eight segments

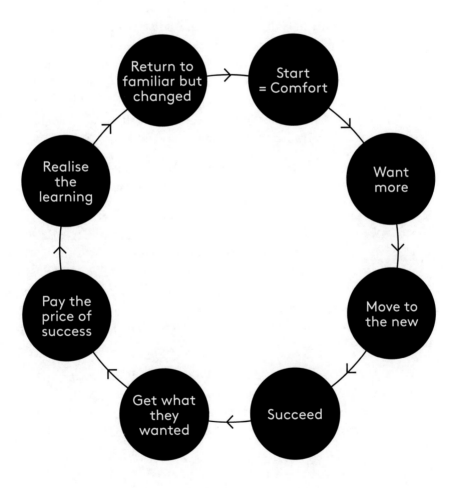

The basic rules of storytelling

1. Work out what you want to say. Identify the key points.
2. Use simple, direct language: cut down on your adjectives. This is the best way to activate the brain regions that relate to the *ideas* in a story.
3. Use emotional words and metaphors, but use them sparingly to let them have impact. Researchers from Emory University have found that when people read a metaphor involving texture, the sensory cortex – the part of the brain responsible for perceiving texture through touch – is activated ("the sharpest scissors," "the jewelled creature," "the crumpled wings").
4. Include the unexpected. Add an element of surprise if you can, to make your story more memorable.
5. Pay attention to the flow of the language. And then go back and make your story simpler. The structure should be engaging but not elaborate.
6. When you come to speak: stand tall, breathe, smile, speak directly and with passion.

If storytelling doesn't come naturally to you, don't worry: you don't have to tell your audience this is a story. Just watch their reaction and see their level of engagement rise.

Louise has been observing people with presence and finds the idea of developing the quality of true presence fits much better with her than trying to acquire some kind of commanding posture and confidence. She's inspired by the fact that a lot of the work in this area is being led by women (she wonders if it was something they had to tackle for themselves). She now sees presence demonstrated by all sorts of people and sees it could improve all her relationships.

Louise prided herself on being the PowerPoint / Prezi queen, but she's now a complete convert to the power of low-tech storytelling and has been enjoying incorporating it in her daily working life. (She has created a goal for herself as well: to do a TED Talk before she's 35!).

Exploring further

Books

Act Like a Leader, Think Like a Leader, Herminia Ibarra

Playing Big, Practical Wisdom for Women Who Want to Speak Up, Create and Lead, Tara Mohr

The Hero with A Thousand Faces (Collected Works of Joseph Campbell), Joseph Campbell

Articles, blogs and podcasts

Simple Acts That Build Your Leadership Presence, Gwen Moran (An inspiring three-minute read.) Fast Company

Owning the Room - Establishing Your Leadership Presence, Karl Moore, Forbes

Videos

Improve Your Leadership Presence, Muriel Maignan Wilkins (The co-author of *Own the Room* defines executive presence in terms of assumptions, communications strategy, and energy.) Harvard Business Review (3:10)

Your body language may shape who you are, Amy Cuddy. (Social psychologist Cuddy shows how "power posing" – standing in a posture of confidence, even when we don't feel confident – can affect testosterone and cortisol levels in the brain, and might even have an impact on our chances for success.) TED.com (21:02)

Charisma, Leadership and the Imposter Syndrome, Olivia Fox Cabane (The author of a guide to charisma says this is not an innate quality and can be learned.) Talks at Google (27:36)

Playing Big: Finding Your Voice, Tara Mohr (Tools and strategies to help women play big.) YouTube (29:21)

This is your brain on communication, Uri Hasson (Neuroscientist Hasson reveals that even across different languages, our brains show similar activity, or become "aligned," when we hear the same idea or story.) TED.com (14:51)

How the Brain Changes Its Mind, Emily Falk (Concealed knowledge in the brain can help predict which types of messages will be most effective in helping people change their behaviour and reach their goals.) TEDx (13:08)

The danger of a single story, Chimamanda Ngozi Adichie (The novelist tells the story of how she found her authentic cultural voice – and warns that if we hear only a single story about another person or country, we risk critical misunderstanding.) TED.com (18:49)

The clues to a great story, Andrew Stanton (The maker of *Toy Story* and *WALL-E* says the essence of storytelling is "make me care".) TED.com (19:16)

Tales of passion, Isabel Allende (The author and activist discusses women, creativity, the definition of feminism and, of course, passion.) TED.com (18:00)

11.
Warm wimp or competent bitch

Life has moved on for Matt and Louise: they are both now successful managers (Louise leading a technical team, Matt heading up a business development team). And they have both recently come back after parental leave: Louise for the first time (she took a year's leave) Matt for the second time (he took three months out). They've had quite different experiences on their return and Louise is keen to compare notes.

Being away from the office gave her time to consider the extra challenges facing women at work. As a technical specialist, she feels she's been insulated from some of the more predictable issues that women face. She realises that her expectations and her relationship with her team may have changed: she's keen to re-establish herself in her role, but she now has less flexibility for working longer hours or socialising after work.

Reflecting on the feedback she's had over the course of her career to date she sees that she started off being told she was too soft and now she may be seen as too tough. She's wondering if women with children are judged more harshly.

Numerous studies have shown that we judge people primarily by two criteria: their warmth, and their competence. The first and most important question we ask ourselves unconsciously when we meet someone is: "Do I *like* this person?" which is an assessment of their warmth and trustworthiness, a reading of their intentions. That's followed by "Do I *respect* this person?" which is a judgement of their effectiveness and competence, and how capable they are of carrying out their intentions.

Likeable or effective: how we judge people

We are constantly assessing people on a scale of warmth vs competence, based on their non-verbal signals. At the same time we are also unintentionally sending a continuous stream of non-verbal signals of our own that other people use to judge how warm or competent *we* are.

These two dimensions account for about 80% of our overall evaluations of people, and shape our behaviour toward them and how we feel about them. This judgement of warmth and competence determines why we hire someone, why we engage easily with one client but not another, even why we may win or lose a piece of business.

Surprisingly, when you ask people how *they* want to be judged, they tend to value competence over warmth. We want *other* people to be warm and trustworthy, but we want *ourselves* to be seen as competent and powerful. We would rather have people respect us than like us.

The importance of warmth

Amy Cuddy from Harvard Business School, who has carried out much of this research with her colleagues, says this is probably a mistake when we consider the importance of social connections to humans. These judgements are made of both men and women, but in the workplace – and especially in considering people in leadership positions or applying for leadership – the judgements come with associations linked to masculine and feminine stereotypes. Masculine leaders are competent and powerful but not warm, feminine leaders are warm but not powerful nor usually seen as competent.

Many leaders demonstrate power but give much less consideration to how much warmth they exhibit. Yet warmth is equated with trust, and we need to connect with people and build trust before we can influence them. Trust is the conduit for influence; it's the medium through which ideas travel. If people don't trust you, they are not going to be open to your ideas. This explains why leaders who rely on command and control may be feared but not trusted, respected but not liked.

"Competence" is for keeps

There's an interesting asymmetry in the assumptions people make about warmth and competence. Many factors can indicate competence: scoring well on an exam, answering a tricky question from a client, getting a good degree, for example. Cuddy's studies have shown that if you demonstrate mastery in one area, it's commonly assumed that you are competent in other, often unrelated areas. This is one reason why technical managers are so commonly appointed to leadership roles (where they often flounder): they have demonstrated their mastery of complex issues that are essential to the success of the organisation. They're *good*: it's assumed they'll be good at people-management as well.

Of course, not all technical managers lack people skills, but without effort and training many fail to add them to their inventory. Louise read a report while she was on maternity leave by the Corporate Executive Board, which researches leadership and business, and learned that 50-70% of executives fail within the first 18 months of promotion into an executive role. (Of those, about 3% "fail spectacularly," while nearly 50% "quietly struggle.") That's not a fate she wants for herself.

There's a sort of "stickiness" to competence: once the label is applied it's not quickly taken away. (Which may be why so many leaders are being left to struggle.) A single incompetent behaviour – failing one exam, one set of poor engagement scores from the team – is not generalised: it will simply be dismissed as a one-off or an unlearned skill. We seem to assume that overall competence can't be faked.

But "kindness" is easily lost

By contrast, warmth (sincerity, trustworthiness...) which is so important to us, is judged differently. And maybe from an evolutionary point of view this was because it was so important to survival: misjudging warmth and trustworthiness could result in death.

A single example of openness, generosity or compassion (helping an elderly person across the street, staying late to help a colleague with a big presentation) will not lead to a generalised assessment that this is a warm, generous, open person. They might just be doing this because it looks like the right thing to do.

But a single instance of being cold or unkind (speaking harshly to a junior staffer, for instance) means they are categorised as an insensitive, heartless person. The assumption seems to be that it's possible to fake warmth or kindness, and a moment of meanness reveals true character.

Women are judged more harshly at work

When Louise wonders if she's being judged more harshly than Matt, is she right?

Pretty much, yes. Because men are more likely to be known for their technical competence than their people skills, and a positive rating for competence and effectiveness is harder to lose, they're effectively given a free pass on their lack of people skills: it's just not expected of them. Their authority and competence is pretty much inviolable. Whereas women are more often promoted for their "warm" people skills, and one miss-step, one incident viewed from an unfavourable angle, can damage their reputation irreparably.

So, a man who didn't anticipate all the technical problems that could arise during the development of a project – that's understandable. But a woman who didn't manage to placate an unhappy client – that's a sign that she doesn't have the right personality for the job.

If you're warm you can't be capable

Louise, of course, runs slightly against stereotype because she has a strong technical background and manages a team of specialists. She's made sure to keep up with the latest research while she's been on maternity leave, and quite reasonably prides herself on her competence and being "up to the job." She's also worked on her people skills. Although she probably under-rates them, and how important they have been to her.

But there's a double-whammy: studies show that people tend to see warmth and competence as inversely related: if someone is seen to be capable, efficient and effective, they're assumed to be less warm and people-oriented. The more competent Louise is seen to be, the more it will be assumed that she's hard-boiled. And now is when she needs her people skills: when she needs to re-establish her leadership, and get her team on board with the fact that she may not be as physically present in the office as she was before.

Women walk the tightrope

Negotiating conflicting expectations at work has been dubbed "the tightrope" by feminist legal scholar Joan Williams and co-author Rachel Dempsey in their book *What works for women at work*. And it's not only women who have to manage this delicate balancing act: men also contend with conflicting expectations.

Walking the tightrope, and trying to combine warmth with competence, means, for Louise, that she's contending with an entrenched understanding that if she were really competent she wouldn't need to be so warm and nice: highly competent people don't have to be liked. In fact, warmth may even be a weakness ("you probably have to step on a few people to get to the top").

Research by Catalyst, the pressure group on equality, found that women leaders were judged as competent *or* liked, but rarely both. Their research showed that when women behave in ways that are traditionally valued for leaders (assertive, authoritative, analytical) they tend to be seen as competent, but they are also seen as less influential, less personable and less effective with people. And they are liked less. And hence less likely to be trusted.

I had a baby, not a lobotomy

To make matters worse for Louise, these judgements on warmth and competence are exaggerated for women who are parents. For mothers, there's a direct trade-off between perceived (we might even say *required*) warmth, and perceived competence. (We *expect* you to be showing the baby photos round the office all the time – *so cute!* – but of course that means you've taken your eye off the job.)

Alison Brittan CEO of UK leisure group Whitbread says people still ask about life work balance, but they mainly ask women. "I have a male colleague with kids the exact same ages as mine and no one asks whether he can balance", she said in an article for LeanIn.org.

But lucky Matt – men gain from becoming fathers. They're now seen as being as warmer, but no less competent.

People who are judged to be more competent get hired and promoted and sent on training courses (even if they're not liked that much). What working mothers gain in perceived warmth they lose on just about every important workplace metric. Employers are less interested in hiring, promoting or training working mothers compared with working fathers or employees without children. And studies show that visibly pregnant women are judged as being less committed to their jobs, less dependable, less authoritative, more emotional, and more irrational than otherwise equal, non-pregnant women.

Are mothers less committed to work?

But perhaps this reflects the reality that mothers really are less committed, and are willing to let things slip a little? A study carried out by Shelley Correll, professor of sociology at Stanford and director of the Clayman Institute for Research on Gender, focused directly on job candidates' competence and commitment levels.

Combining laboratory experiments with assessments by participants, and an audit of actual employers, Correll found that that even if mothers *were* unambiguously committed and competent, they were still discriminated against:

> • Mothers were considered to be *less* committed to their jobs than non-mothers.
> • Fathers were perceived as being 5 percentage points *more* committed than non-fathers (the "breadwinner" assumption?).
> • Childless women were eight times more likely to be recommended for a promotion than mothers.
> • Childless women are offered twice as many interviews as equally qualified mothers.
> • Mothers are held to higher punctuality standards: on average, they were allowed to be late 3.16 days per month, while childless women were allowed to be late on 3.73 days.
> • Fathers were allowed to have *more* days late than non-fathers: 3.6 days per month compared to 3.16 days.
> • Fathers are offered significantly higher starting salaries than childless men.
> • Mothers are recommended for 7.9% *lower* starting salaries than non-mothers, which were already lower than salaries for fathers and childless men.

Most disappointingly, female participants were the ones who gave female candidates the lowest ratings. The Stanford researchers say the "motherhood penalty" may account for a significant proportion of the gender gap in pay.

Stereotypes become self-fulfilling prophecies

Being penalised in this stereotyped way can have the dangerous effect of leading women to doubt their own competence, and that in turn can have a measurable impact on their performance. "This is how self-fulfilling prophecies work," says social psychologist Amy Cuddy: "We have an expectation about who someone is and how she's likely to behave, then we treat her in a way that is likely to elicit those behaviours, thus confirming our initial expectations... and so on."

Psychologist Claude Steele from UC Berkeley has shown that when women start doubting their skills due to these perceptions, their actual performance also suffers. And the effect is strongest, unsurprisingly, in settings where gender stereotypes are strongest, and where women hear comments such as "Oh, goodness she's pregnant: that's going to cost us" every day.

Hanging on to the most effective behaviours

The problem with judgements about how men and women "should" behave is that they separate traits which could work together to produce much better results at work. For men as well as women, authority exercised with warmth is better than command and control.

What's troubling about a traditional definition of femininity is that it assumes warmth also means a kind of submissiveness and reduced competence: "She's really good with the graduates but we can't have her working with the partners - they would just walk all over her." Having more role models showing what femininity linked with authority can look like would take us a long way in business. "She really connects and cares about her people but won't allow slacking. She expects everyone to contribute."

Combining "masculine competence" and "feminine niceness"

And what about the traits of compassion and connection? The stereotyped assumption is that women leaders are naturally more communal in their leadership style, that they're relationship-oriented and sympathetic to other people's needs. But Williams' and Dempsey's research for *What works for women at work*, and also the Head Heart + Brain research have shown that female leaders are communal not by nature but by necessity. They can't just rely on their technical skills. Relationships get things done in complex matrix organisations. They behave empathetically because they sense, accurately, that what works for women is a style that mixes masculine competence with feminine niceness.

One research participant in STEM told us her technical skills alone could not get her onto a high-profile project, but when the team started having relationship issues she was co-opted on because it was assumed that she was good at understanding others and collaborating. The command-and-control strategy that can work for men is often still risky for women, and with what we know about the brain, not very effective. People can be threatened into action but it comes with reduced cognitive processing power, creativity and problem solving.

Pick your moments of super-competence

Walking the tightrope, says Amy Cuddy, may not mean surrendering to the stereotype. For example, people, especially leaders, tend to overemphasise the importance of projecting high competence. In particular, traditional male leaders want to be the smartest person in the room, she says. Clearly there are advantages to being seen as highly competent – the research shows you will in turn feel more powerful and more willing to take risks.

But it's rarely a good idea to be like that all the time. It alienates people, makes them defensive about their own status and thus less receptive to influence and new ideas. And if you're preoccupied with appearing competent and powerful there isn't the mental capacity to also be creative, and to read other people and what they need.

Pick and choose your moments of shining brilliance is Cuddy's recommendation. Your goal should be *to connect with people* first and only impress them with your abilities occasionally. They are much more likely to listen to and believe your ideas if they already like and trust you.

Finding the balance

Achieving a balance between competence and warmth is, for many women, a daily juggling act. In our research women told us that the kinds of experiences they really struggle with are:

- A choice that leaves you confused about whether you want to be at home with your family or pursuing your career - an offer of promotion which requires longer hours just as you are returning from maternity leave.
- A conversation that feels staged, the person is being unclear about what they really mean. This is even more disturbing when there is no rapport. An HR manager asking you how you feel about a new role that requires travel but never articulates if there is a concen "How are you feeling about going to Hong Kong every quarter?"
- A mistake that makes you question who you really are. Like choosing the trip with a client over your toddler's first nursery school play.

Resolving these internal conflicts requires a strong sense of self: what researchers call "self-concept clarity." When you know who you are you experience greater self-esteem, clarity and independence, the research shows. Self-concept clarity also helps you to create better relationships and a sense of purpose in life and work.

Achieving "self-concept clarity"

It sounds great, and we can recognise it when we see it in other people, but how do you develop it? A new study looking at the benefits of mindfulness (such as reduced stress and improved wellbeing) sought to understand what actually brings about these changes.

Adam Hanley at the University of Utah's Centre on Mindfulness and Integrative Health asked over 1,000 undergraduate students (ranging in age from 18 to 53) to complete questionnaires about three traits:

Mindfulness: Their tendency to be aware of their present thoughts and feelings and to respond to them in deliberate, non-reactive, non-judgmental ways.
Self-concept clarity: How stable, clear, and un-conflicted their views of themselves are.

Wellbeing: How much they feel a sense of self-acceptance, autonomy, and control over their environment; the quality of their relationships; and their experience of personal growth and purpose in life.

As you'd expect, the results showed that the more mindful participants reported higher wellbeing—and that stronger sense of self partly accounted for the effect. But some aspects of mindfulness were more important than others. Participants who were *non-judgmental* about their thoughts and feelings tended to report a particularly clear sense of self. Those who were better at *observing* their thoughts and feelings had slightly lower self-concept clarity.

Awareness, it seems, is not enough: a degree of acceptance is vital. "Being non-judgmental may increase the likelihood of accepting how you feel about yourself," says Hanley, "which may increase the willingness of more mindful individuals to explore and examine the self – ultimately, being more familiar or friendly with themselves." In other words, if you notice your flaws but don't beat yourself up for them, you are more willing to be honest with yourself about your strengths and weaknesses, and accept yourself as you are.

Using mindfulness to trigger change

We talk about mindfulness throughout this book and increasingly women, and men, are finding that being mindful helps them to notice how they are being treated and what stereotypes are at work, and to have more control over whether they work along with those stereotypes, or challenge them. Mindfulness is really a prerequisite for making change: you can only change your situation when you're aware of what's going on.

And the motivation to change is largely determined by whether you are getting the results you want. If being warm, likeable and trustworthy (but perhaps a bit of a pushover) works for you, why would you change? But if being a bit of a soft touch means that actually you're imposed upon and taken for granted, and your time isn't valued as highly as other people's, you might want to do things differently.

Understanding how other people perceive you, and the impact of your behaviour, are all mindful acts. Having clarity, especially when your personal circumstances change, is a powerful product of practising mindfulness.

Reduce inner conflict

The reduced uncertainty and conflict of self-doubt can allow you to confidently pursue goals and relationships that are most important to you. And if you are mindful and notice the changes and improvements in yourself it can help to let go of ingrained beliefs that are no longer true, such as "I'm just not an assertive person," or "I'm too junior to speak up in that meeting."

A strong self-concept is vital in a world that is constantly changing, and particularly when you're making major life and career changes. The more clarity you have about who you are and what is important to you, the more confident you can be in your decisions.

Adam Hanley's research doesn't prove that mindfulness *causes* us to develop a stronger sense of self, but it does show a connection. In the meantime, given the other well-documented benefits of mindfulness, taking up the practice isn't going to do you any harm.

Career hacks

What image do you project?

If, as a woman, you're judged to be strongly feminine (too warm) you may attract labels like gentle, nice or soft-hearted. If you're judged to be strongly masculine you'll hear yourself described as aggressive, competitive, forceful or individualistic. Spot the difference? When these masculine labels are applied to men they're a compliment but when applied to women they're more often a criticism.

Find out how you're perceived:

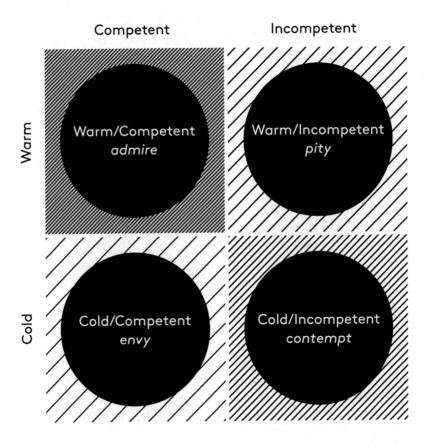

First rate yourself based on your intuition.

Then use actual examples of how you have behaved: in a range of work situations and plot where the behaviours would fall on the graph. Examples might be:

- How you've reacted in a crisis
- How you react under deadline pressure
- How you've related to your team at a time of stress
- How you relate to your team when all is going well
- How you interact with people more senior to you
- How you are on a typical day
- How you interact with people junior to you

Compare where your behavioural examples fall on the grid to where you positioned yourself based on your intuition. If there is a difference think about why that may be:

- Did you only think of one of the examples above?
- Did you only consider the good days/people or the bad days or with challenging people?
- Are you relating to different types of people in each situation?

Then ask a few friends and trusted colleagues where they would place you (don't tell them too much about the background research, or your own self-assessment). Ask for their examples. (You might find this is an entertaining exercise to do amongst a group of friends over drinks. Or you could introduce it as a workshop exercise on a team training day.)

Is there a difference between how you're perceived by colleagues at work, and how friends and family see you at home? Think about why this is: do you adopt a different persona at work? Are you warmer with family? How can you transfer some of that warmth to colleagues?

The next step is to notice if these work habits are serving you well:

- What do you show most of and in what context?
- Are you warmer in some situations than others?
- When would it be helpful to show more competence?
- Do you need to increase warmth or perceptions of competence overall?

Once you have decided how warm or how competent you want to be in a given situation, a meeting or a presentation, say, set out your plan. (You might want to read the "becoming more self-aware section on how different behaviours are perceived – you'll find them below.)

Become more self-aware

We believe that being self-aware is essential to working more effectively, and being happier and more fulfilled in your work – whether you're a man or a woman. Being *mindful* of what is going on in your day-to-day work is one way of increasing self-awareness; without awareness, you are blind to the things that have an impact on you and your performance.

We all get into habits of behaving in particular ways with different people, for example displaying warm and low-competence behaviours (low status) with an old boss even though you are now equals. Or using high-competence behaviours when you're nervous, even though you want to connect with a new colleague.

Actors make use of physiology and behaviours to signal warmth and competence (in stage-craft they're typically called status behaviours) and there's a lot we can learn from them.

Keep a warmth / coolness diary

One tool is to keep a log of how you behave with a particular person, especially someone who you need to work with in a different way because you're not getting the results you want. Notice all the subtle ways you behave – many of them will have become habits and it will take a bit of effort to notice them. Consider how you hold your body, your movements, and how you speak. These behaviours signal your warmth and competent and how you will be perceived.

You can combine this with the feedback you get from the exercise above. The list of behaviours below can act as a guide. If you have trouble being mindful of your own habits (after all they are often not conscious behaviours) ask a trusted colleague to help you to keep a log of your behaviour. Take a look also at the video mentioned below for examples (somewhat exaggerated) of what each behaviour looks like.

Behaviours which signal low competence and which tend to be perceived as warmth	Behaviours which signal high competence and which tend to be perceived as cool
When walking, you move out of another person's path first	You move comfortably, taking control of your own space
You sit or stand compactly, with arms folded across your body, feet tucked under the chair. If tall, you slouch	You spread out your body and take up space: legs splayed, arms behind your head or draped along someone's chair
You avoid looking into another person's eyes	You make eye contact when speaking
You fidget and make unnecessary movements: touching face and hair, fiddling with jewellery	Your movements are minimal – deliberate and purposeful gestures
You literally look up to the other person. If you are short you stand further away	You talk casually about things you know the other person finds important
You easily get emotional	You restrict your reactions and facial expressions
You tend to speak hesitantly in incomplete sentences punctuated with umm's and aah's	You speak in complete sentences, briefly and at an even pace
You monitor the other person's reaction as you speak	You avoid looking at other people's reactions
You're always careful to explain any jargon or "in talk"	You like using jargon and "in talk": it conveys expertise
You fudge your words when having "difficult" discussions, to avoid the issue	You give direct feedback on the person's work or contribution, especially in public
You avoid making decisions for the group. You defer to other people even when you have the expertise	You make decisions for the group

Once you have collected data over a few meetings look at the trends and notice how you position yourself with the person. Are you using more high-competence or low-competence behaviours? And which would be most useful to get the outcome you want? (Bear in mind it's not always a good idea to be high-status all the time.)

Now consider what small changes you can make to get closer to your desired outcome? And monitor the results you get.

For example, if you typically use high-competence behaviours with clients, warm up a bit by adopting one or two low-competence behaviours. Looking for their the reaction is important (you will probably need to do this over a period of time rather than at just one meeting). It's best to make one change at a time to avoid getting overwhelmed.

Show your potential as much as your achievements

And finally, when the stakes are high it's easy to assume that the best way to project competence is to focus on letting people know about your achievements and experience. But Zakary Tormala of Stanford Graduate School has demonstrated a powerful unconscious bias for potential over actual success.

In one study participants were given statistical data on NBA players which was described as either the player's actual record or their projected capability. Participants said they would pay more for the players with potential than those who they had the actual data for. And the same pattern was found with job applicants.

The Stanford researchers believe this bias exists because the human brain pays more attention to uncertainty when it encounters it, and wants to sort out the data to be more certain. Data on potential makes us think harder, and leaders unconsciously form a more positive judgement. The clear indication is that you should practise talking about "you in the future": what you *can* do (rather than what you already do) and how you will do it.

Returning from maternity leave it has been shocking for Louise to learn how the double standards for women (and especially working mothers) could affect her own pay and prospects. However, forewarned is forearmed, she reckons. Her established reputation for technical competence is a help, but she'll need to avoid wanting to be the smartest person in the room all the time. What she needs to develop now are her warm people skills to help her over this tricky transition.

She's making a conscious effort not to be too busy to connect with her team-members on a personal level, and she's made a commitment to socialise with them after work at least once a month. And while she had practised mindfulness earlier in her career she is now determined to get back into it. She needs to be confident of her self-concept to manage this transition to motherhood and more senior roles. And to be mindful of the reactions of other people as well.

Exploring further

Books

What Works for Women at Work: Four Patterns Working Women Need to Know, Joan Williams and Rachel Dempsey

Articles, blogs and podcasts

Connect, Then Lead, Amy Cuddy, Matthew Kohut, and John Neffinger (Is it better to be loved or feared? To exert influence, we need to balance competence with warmth.) Harvard Business Review

Women Rising: the Unseen Barriers, Herminia Ibarra, Robin J. Ely and Deborah M. Kolb, Harvard Business Review. (The authors argue that to manage the competence-likability trade-off women leaders to be sure of their sense of purpose.)

To Seem Confident, Women Have to be Seen as Warm, Margarita Mayo, Harvard Business Review. 2016 (Details of a study that says to be promoted women need to be seen as competent, confident and warm)

Videos

Measuring Trust: Through Competence – or Warmth? Adam Waytz (When businesses try to build trust, they typically focus on competence, which can be quantified. Warmth seems much less measurable.) The Trust Project at Northwestern University (3:33)

The HUMAN Brand: How We Relate to People, Products, and Companies, Susan Fiske and Chris Malone. (Why do you like Coke and not Pepsi? Honda and not Toyota? Why we make the choices we do.) YouTube (46:41)

Can we 'have it all'? Anne-Marie Slaughter TED. Com. (Here Slaughter expands her ideas and explains why shifts in work culture, public policy and social mores can lead to more equality — for men, women, all of us.) (17mins, 07secs)

12.
Own your ambition

Meet Meena and Jay who've been at Multinational Trading for around 10 years and have become friends through their shared interest in a neuroscience approach to their leadership. Compared with many of the male leaders in the company, Jay is a bit more considerate and less pushy; nonetheless he has come to the attention of the CEO and is being groomed for a divisional director role.

Meena is ambitious; she's taken care of her relationships and networking. She's aware that she's not progressing as fast as Jay, and while she doesn't want to blame it on gender discrimination she's beginning to think that's the issue. For her, it's a daily juggling act managing work and family. Jay has children too, and is a very committed parent, but he doesn't seem to find the competing demands draining in the same way that Meena does.

She currently has very little time to think strategically about her career: she's too busy getting on with the job. Has she been "passed over" for higher management? If that's the case she's wondering if she should just downsize her ambitions, at least until her children are older.

There's no progress without ambition, no triumph without drive, determination and commitment. Or so a conventionally masculine model of corporate success would have us believe. Women, like men, experience reward and pleasure from doing things well. We're not planning and strategizing, working long hours and sacrificing time away from our family just to help others and to be "nice". We know – most of us – that opportunities and promotion are not going to come to those who sit back and wait.

But the idea of "being driven," or "relentless ambition" may not sit well with many women. We know we need to be seen to be ambitious to be taken seriously, but... not so much that we stop being true to ourselves, or re-write every idea of what it means to be a woman.

Can we be feminine *and* ambitious?

"When you say 'ambitious woman' there's a judgy tinge to it that doesn't happen for men," says *New York Times* writer and author Stephanie Clifford, talking about her novel *Everybody Rise* in which an ambitious women loses sight of herself. "If all you hear about a woman is that she's ambitious, you probably wouldn't want to hang out with her."

The question is essentially: can we be ambitious and remain true to ourselves? Can we strive to achieve our goals as women, or do we have to acquire all the power-suit characteristics of men. Do we *want* to be described as "relentlessly ambitious" (a description that might not have a successful man struck off the dinner-guest list)? Well, when you put it like that... it seems quite a believable stereotype that many women just aren't as driven. And understand-able (if regrettable) that this is one of the major obstacles to gender equality.

Opting out... or redefining?

Are many of us just not ruthlessly ambitious in the same way as men? Or is it just that we don't want to own the label – but are qui-etly prepared to do everything that's needed to make it to the top? Or do we perhaps understand quite clearly that to exhibit male-type ambitious behaviour would be to invite open hostility?

Ann Sherry, executive chairman of Carnival, the leading cruise op-erator in Australasia, says: "When I first started work, I did what a lot of women do, which is I tried to fit the mould: to look, sound, and feel the same way as others. That was probably my first epiph-any, early in my career: I stopped and thought, 'What is going on?' That feeling has stayed with me forever. Once I made a conscious decision to be clear to everyone that 'This is who I am,' it felt like a huge load had been lifted."

It's astonishing how many high-profile women don't own their ambition easily. Emma Walmsley, CEO of GlaxoSmithKline, says "I'm starting to be convinced I have a right to be at the top table in business and am genuinely happy in my new company where I know I'm making a difference."

Certainly, many women in the Head Heart + Brain research were reluctant to admit to it. When asked directly how ambitious they were, the typical responses were:

"I'm not really ambitious – I just like to do a good job."
"I hate to promote myself, my work should stand for itself."
"It's not about me; it's about…"

We also heard the term used as a criticism. One (female) government employee, talking about the appointment of a new director said: "She's very ambitious you know." (With a raise of her eyebrows and a tone that suggested this was an issue.)

This is a uniquely female way of speaking about ambition: men do not say these things. And what's important is that these responses come from very successful women who are senior in their careers, who might be expected to have acquired sufficient power, or self-confidence, or allies in the organisation, or a thick-enough skin, to own their ambition. Which suggests that their reluctance to broadcast it is born of experience, and is perhaps a wise camouflage strategy.

Mastery requires recognition

Researching what ambition actually means to women, psychiatrist Anna Fels, author of *Necessary Dreams: Ambition in Women's Changing Lives*, found that women disliked describing themselves as ambitious now, but were happy to talk about their childhood ambitions. She found there was a common pattern to how they described these childhood dreams: their descriptions involved mastery of a skill or ability and being known for that mastery – being recognised by someone, usually many people, for it.

We know that as humans we get a sense of reward and pleasure for doing things well. But mastery demands motivation to keep going, and support and appreciation over time to maintain the effort and encourage us to overcome obstacles and setbacks.

In fact, it may not be possible for anyone to achieve their dreams as a loner. A longitudinal study led by Harvard psychologist Jerome Kagan examined the relationship between striving for mastery and receiving recognition for achieving the goals and skills. Following a group from childhood, the conclusion was that there is a high correlation between mastery and recognition: "It may be impossible to measure the desire to improve a skill independent of the individual's desire for recognition."

The problem is that if women's achievements are ignored or undervalued, we may never manage to push on to achieve our fullest potential.

Why aren't women at the centre of their own success?

Anna Fels identifies another obstacle for women when we look at the commonly agreed traits of femininity as defined in the Bem Sex Role Inventory (BSRI) (the standard test used for assessing gender roles developed at Stamford by the late psychologist Sandra Bem). The 20 feminine characteristics are (apart from "feminine"): yielding, loyal, cheerful, compassionate, shy, sympathetic, affectionate, sensitive to the needs of others, flatterable, understanding, eager to soothe hurt feelings, soft-spoken, warm, tender, gullible, child-like, does not use harsh language, gentle and loves children. As Fels points out, they are all about support and relationships.

By contrast, the agreed BSRI characteristics of masculinity are largely self-determined: masculine, self-reliant, strong personality, forceful, independent, analytical, defends one's beliefs, athletic, assertive, has leadership abilities, willing to take risks, makes decisions easily, self-sufficient, dominant, willing to take a stand, aggressive, acts as a leader, individualistic, competitive and... ambitious.

Men, it seems, can be masculine by themselves; women cannot be feminine without being reflected in the eyes of other people. This may be why women do not set themselves at the centre of their success, and we hear so many women attributing their success not to mastery and recognition but to luck.

The family dilemma

In practice people can and do mix these feminine and masculine traits, and there are many situations in which they are compatible and even complementary. You can, for example, be a strong leader who is sensitive and responsive to the needs of your team.

But there are also circumstances in which the traits inevitably collide, and not least when men and women are in competition with each other at work, and when they start to build their families. Increasingly precious and limited resources must be allocated: time for work, for leisure, for financial independence, for career advancement, and for power.

Here you might experience clashes over the feminine needs for talking and collaborating and the masculine needs for driving decisions; or between the feminine need to nurture and the masculine need to take control. As we know, these can impact everything from holiday choice to how you bring up children.

Allocating personal resources

Women must decide how to allocate resources (essentially their own time, focus and energy) to family, to support of their partner and their partner's career, and to their own work. Which potentially leaves very little time and focus for their own career ambitions.

Managing the balance successfully can take a phenomenal amount of organisation and commitment. A partner in a consulting firm told us how she and her partner had meticulously planned their support structure around her career once she realised she could make partner in her firm. Her husband provided support while she worked all-out, and now she is a partner and going off on maternity leave she can support him and his work for a while.

Challenges to ambition

Women experience (or notice) the most social and organisational discrimination during their late twenties and early thirties, when they are starting to compete seriously with men. These are the career stages where people make the jump (if they are going to) into roles where they need to influence others, not just be responsible for their own work. This is also at the age when women most frequently marry and have children. With all of these pressures they must decide whether to try to hold on to their own ambitions or downsize or abandon them.

Current research suggests that in order to be seen as feminine, women must provide or relinquish resources – including recognition of their accomplishments and skills, and their time and energy – to others. Women already experience more negative feedback in very ordinary social and work interactions. In one study, for example, male and female study participants took turns assuming leader and non-leader roles whilst performing a problem-solving task. The researchers found that regardless of which role the woman took, they received more negative facial reactions than positive ones.

It's different amongst women

A bit of glum-face and eye-rolling doesn't sound too serious. But experienced day in and day out it serves to depress women's judgements of the value of their contributions and their prospects of doing well. It certainly doesn't provide recognition to motivate ongoing mastery.

And research demonstrates the social context is crucial: women will be much more open about seeking and competing for appreciation and recognition when they are with other women – such as all-girls schools, or women's sports teams (who can forget the Team GB women's hockey team's victory lap after their gold medal win in Rio?). And they have no reluctance in seeking out and starring in roles that complement rather than compete with men – including, literally, starring on stage and screen. But women are socialised to modify their behaviour when they are competing *directly* with men: toning down the high-fives and the whoop-whoops to avoid criticism.

Are we becoming more ambitious?

There is mixed evidence about whether things are getting better, and women are outgrowing this socialised behaviour to hold back on ambition. College women in the US have been shown to be identifying more with masculine traits than they have in the past – without losing any of their female identity. They share goals such as becoming an authority in their line of work, obtaining recognition from colleagues, and being financially successful.

A survey by the Boston Consulting Group (BCG) of 200,000 employees, including 141,000 women from 189 countries, found women are just as ambitious as men at the outset of their careers, and their ambitions were constrained not by family status or motherhood but by their organisations.

BCG found that among employees aged under 30 there was little difference in ambition between men and women. And consistent with the argument that women down play their ambition when they need to give energy to home and family, the research found the strength of ambition waned in both sexes over time, but women's ambition eroded significantly faster than men's and (predictably) faster at organisations with a poor record of gender diversity.

Closing the gap

The ambition gap between women and men aged 30 to 40 was 17 % at organisations that were rated as least progressive on gender diversity, and at these places only 66% of women sought promotion (compared with 83% of men).

But at organisations where there was almost no ambition gap between women and men aged 30 to 40, 85% of women sought promotion, compared with 87% of men. Matt Krentz, co-author of the report, believes this shows: "Ambition is not a fixed trait; it is an attribute that can be nurtured or damaged over time through the daily interactions and opportunities employees experience at work."

Some structural changes would help!

Another reason women give for not striving for the top is the lack of organisational support. Most companies are still designed around an assumption that someone else takes care of home and family life. And – ironically – the networking opportunities which might be a powerful encouragement to working women also often follow these unthinking stereotypes.

As one woman told the Head Heart + Brain survey: "There need to be better ways to help women create a network other than after-work drinks or dinner. If that remains the primary networking tool, women are never going to get to the C-suite, because that's not the choice they're going to make."

The media are quick to highlight every example of a high-achieving woman who walks away from a top job, shedding column-inches of crocodile tears over the relentless demands made of corporate high-fliers (but sending a clear message that women somehow just can't cut it).

Finding an alternative path

But perhaps there are subtler reasons why women step off the conventional career ladder. Shelley Wright Brindle, the former Executive Vice President of HBO, says she decided to leave not because she wasn't successful there but because she wanted to define success on her own terms. The mother of three children still at home, she says she's learned that working mothers do better in organisations that value outcomes rather than long hours in the office.

For some women, the very problems they have faced have created alternative career opportunities: start-ups like Digital Mums, which teaches stay-at-home mothers to use social media skills to create businesses they can fit with family obligations, and PowerToFly, a web-based employment service for women who want to work remotely.

"Women aren't being less ambitious," says Katharine Zaleski, who started PowerToFly with Milena Berry. "They are just unable to commit to a structure that was set up for 50% of the population." Launched just a year ago, their company has connected women to jobs in 43 countries. And Mae O'Malley, a former Google contract lawyer, established Paragon Legal with the same idea, and her San Francisco firm now employs almost 70 lawyers, most of them women looking for ways to make their careers fit their lives, not vice versa.

And this is no longer an issue just for women: a 2014 Harvard Business School study of more than 6,500 HBS graduates showed that men are more family-focused than ever before: a third of male millennials expect to split child care 50-50, compared with 22% of Gen X men and 16% of boomer men. And a quarter of men cited "flexible hours" and "supportive environment" as most important attributes in their workplace. How ironic if it's only when men join battle on this that significant changes will start to be made.

Career hacks

Build your own support network

Women who make it to the top frequently mention how important it has been to have a supportive, encouraging network around them. Your achievements won't always win the plaudits they deserve:

- Really acknowledge the importance of this kind of recognition for your talents and work.
- Do a critical assessment of your "spheres of recognition" that can provide this affirmation.
- If you don't have a strong support team, go out and find the people who make you feel good, a women's network, or a friendship group.
- Recognition and praise are vital for maintaining motivation: make an effort to provide this for other women at work.
- Give yourself a pat on the back or reward when you achieve something substantial. One highly successful women told us she always buys herself a treat: a new piece of jewellery, an expensive handbag and even one time a statue, when she achieves a significant goal or promotion.
- Make a point of sending occasional emails praising particular achievements – or praising the kind of dogged determination that can go unnoticed. (You could include men, but make sure that women are generously featured.)
- Recruit some organisational support from an influential leader, or HR, for a professional women's support group in your workplace. Invite along some inspiring speakers. And make sure that it's accessible and welcoming to working mothers.

Find mentors and sponsors

- Hard work and high achievement is not enough to get you where you want to be. Even if you're not battling against active discrimination at work, women have much more difficulty than men developing relationships with people who have the power to advance their careers. Finding mentors and sponsors does not come naturally to most women but they will be essential to you.

Imagine your future

• Because so little is mapped out for women, you need to actively imagine yourself into the future (there are fewer role models to inspire us and show us the way). Use the power of *envisioning* used by successful sports people, rehearsing a mental picture of themselves holding the trophy aloft before an important match.

• Women also have too *many* roles: innovative professional, independent wage-earner, caring mother, efficient employee, supportive partner, design-savvy homemaker... And many of these roles conflict with what's expected in senior jobs and leadership at work. It falls nearly entirely on you, as a woman, to carve out a life for yourself with adequate meaning and satisfaction: (not an easy task for anyone!). For women more than men, life needs a clear purpose, with values, priorities, and a clear sense of identity.

Meena feels a bit feistier now about how women's ambition is shaped and supported – or fails to be supported. She's prepared to see this less as a result of her own character and lack of personal determination, and more of a system failure. When she sees how Jay, once her equal, is not letting the same considerations hold him back, she's more determined to make time for the supportive networks she knows she really needs to help her to push on at this stage. She's aware she will need to prioritise this in her increasingly complex life.

At the same time, Meena feels more confident about re-framing success in her own terms. She's looking for inspiring role models who have managed to combine work and family with their own personal values.

Exploring further

Books

Necessary Dreams: Ambition in Women's Changing Lives, Anna Fels

Lean In: Women, Work, and the Will to Lead, Sheryl Sandberg

Articles, blogs and podcasts

The Ambition Interviews, Rebecca Rosen (Seven stories about women who were all set to rule the world – and how their careers turned out.) The Atlantic

Why Women Vanish as They Move Up The Career Ladder, Bob Sherwin (Leadership consultant Sherwin examines women's leadership effectiveness, representation in corporate America, and solutions for increasing their ranks.) Business Insider

Balancing Parenting and Work Stress: A Guide, Daisy Wademan Dowling (The 10 best-of empowering and often surprising advice tips for working parents, including: if you want flexibility at work, don't just ask – sell the idea.) Harvard Business Review

Do women lack ambition? Anna Fels (Women more openly seek and compete for affirmation when they are with other women. They face the reality that to appear feminine they must provide or relinquish scarce resources to others—and recognition is a scarce resource.) Harvard Business Review

The Times Top 50 Employers for Women 2017 (UK)

Top Companies For Women Executives In 2017, Karsten Strauss, Forbes magazine

Closing the gender gap needs support from the boss, Sarah Gordon (Three multinationals show how corporate leadership is critical to achieve diversity.) Financial Times

Videos

What's Draining Women's Ambition? Orit Gadiesh and Julie Coffman (After just two years on the job, women's aspirations and confidence to reach senior management plummet compared to men's.) Harvard Business Review Video (1:27)

13.
Why women *still* have to perform better than men

Jay is being interviewed for a position as a director of a business unit in the company. After that he'll only be one step away from the management committee; he's already getting to meet with some of them when presenting data on the best performance results in the organisation that he and Meena have been achieving as a result of their neuroscience-based approach to team management.

He's pleased that her results mirror his own: it's stronger evidence supporting their approach, and also allows him to be a good friend in promoting her achievement.

But no-one's asking Meena to present on her results: is she being unreasonable when she wonders what she needs to do to make herself equally visible? Her team is highly effective and she has had good 360 leadership survey feedback. But it doesn't seem to be enough...

If anyone doubts that double standards still permeate the most powerful and innovative organisations around the world, whose testimony could be more persuasive than a Stanford scientist who used to be a woman – and is now a man?

Ben Barres, professor of neurobiology of Stanford University School of Medicine was born Barbara Barres. He began his sex change process at the age of 40 and was concerned that it might seriously harm his scientific career. He was not aware of any change in cognitive function or emotion, and says that his colleagues at Stanford, nationally and internationally have all been very supportive. But by far the biggest difference he has noticed is that "people who do not know that I was a woman treat me with far more respect. I can even complete a whole sentence without being interrupted by a man."

Colleagues even went as far as judging his work to be better. One commented that Ben's research was so much better than his sister's (having assumed that was who had carried out the research in his female name). Another colleague told him he had never met a woman who was a capable neurosurgeon. And the reverse effect has been reported by men who have transitioned to be women who have suddenly found their competence and capability being questioned.

Ben Barres' experiences have made him vividly aware of gender-based stereotypes. He comments that the only other time he's taken action that he thought might harm his career was when he started fighting for the welfare of women in academia.

The double standards that women have to contend with take a variety of forms.

239

Micro messages

Many women say they didn't notice how the double standards operated in their organisation until they were well into their careers. The behaviour is subtle: it's not a brickbat, or a door slammed in your face. But research indicates that even apparently insignificant behaviours can have a potent and cumulative effect on women's upward progress.

Many of these damagingly insidious prejudices are communicated by micro-messages. Small acts, even apparently benevolent ones, can create a powerful sense of exclusion: a slight raising of the eyebrows expressing doubt, an impatient tone of voice, speaking over a woman, not correcting men who are taking credit for a woman's input. Videos available online (see Exploring further) demonstrate these vividly. All of these seemingly small behaviours can make a woman doubt she has the support of her leader. That's when women stop contributing to group discussions, they become less visible and eventually their performance slips.

In a 2013 interview with Harvard Business Review, Facebook COO Sheryl Sandberg enumerated damaging examples of micro-messaging such as taking more questions from men than women, interrupting women more often than men, and expressing surprise or doubt (even unwittingly) about a female colleague's career aspirations.

Mary Rowe, a professor at the Sloan School of management at MIT was the first to define such gestures in 1972 as "micro-inequities" and acknowledged that victims, bystanders and leaders alike find it hard to identify them. When the targets of micro-inequities do recognise the micro-messages, they find it's exceedingly hard to explain to other people why these small behaviours can be a huge problem. They are small behaviours: it's easy to belittle their effect.

And responding in a large way, by calling out the behaviour when it occurs ("You have your back turned towards me, Greg, when you're addressing the group") can create a sense of nit-picking awkwardness that's hard to recover from.

Micro-responses

Micro-behaviours call for equally subtle micro-responses. The speaker has positioned themselves so their back is towards you? Walk around to be in their clear line of sight. Someone's talking over you in a meeting? Make a gesture that clearly signals waiting (hands together, palm to palm underneath your chin, or sit with elbow on table, one finger raised, pointing upwards to "reserve" conversational space).

Rowe and more recent researchers have also found that there were some gestures that have a positive impact; she termed these micro-affirmations. Micro-affirmations are tiny acts of helping, signalling an interrupter to wait, smiling and nodding, opening the circle to allow someone to join it. They can be very powerful: by simply asking the opinion of a female colleague in a group discussion, leaders can exhibit micro-affirmations that raise self-esteem and social reputation. And when groups see the leader doing this, the behaviour spreads and others start adopting similar micro-affirmations.

Prove it again, and again

Confirmation bias is the well-recognised psychological pattern in which information which serves to confirm a stereotype is noted, while information that contradicts a stereotype is dismissed. For women, it plays out as the "prove it again" effect. In the research for their book *What Works for Women* Joan Williams and Rachel Dempsey found that over two-thirds of women recognised it as having happened to them.

For example: women appear to be more of a risk for high-profile jobs because their appointment contradicts the stereotype (there are fewer examples of women to point to who have been successful and many more men). So women must demonstrate more experience, a higher level of performance and show more competence and dedication to get the same promotions as a man. Men only have to prove their competence once; women must prove theirs again and again.

Here are some examples of how the bias plays out.

More experience needed for pay increases

It's commonly believed that one of the most effective ways to increase pay is to move employers: Catalyst, the international non-profit organisation with a mission to accelerate progress for women in the workplace, have found that men in their second job after completing an MBA were earning $14,000 more than in their first job.

But there is no equivalent advantage for employer mobility for women. Women who stay with an employer do better than those who move employers because women are rewarded based on their experience whilst men are rewarded or hired based on their potential. Staying with the same employer helps woman to point to evidence of their experience.

More experience needed for promotion

And women need to be better to get promoted. One HR director in the Head Heart + Brain research said she sees this in the process for appointing partners in law firms. Male candidates for partner are given the benefit of the doubt and their applications are pushed through by sponsors. For women, there is no such leg-up. The conversation will focus on the experience she lacks or the gaps in her track record, rather than what she has achieved, as with male candidates. More often than not her application will be pushed back for another year.

Other respondents reported that a man gets sponsorship if he is seen to have potential. A woman needs to have a proven client track record and experience.

In another study by Catalyst almost 40% of interviewees mentioned the expectation for women to have more experience and to "tick all the boxes" as an additional hurdle for women that slowed promotion. When asked whether men and women leaders are held to different standards, many participants in the research agreed that they were.

One woman executive observed: "I've come to believe over the years... that we have to work to a different standard. I truly believe that women and minorities work against a different standard." And a woman manager in Europe said: "Men and women are seen differently, and the difference in my experience and observation is that we (women) need to show it (competence) more times before they believe it. With a woman, they will want to see the behaviour repeated more frequently before they will say that this is really part of the woman's capabilities."

A few respondents in the Catalyst study viewed the additional effort expected in positive terms: "Women leaders have shown themselves to be quick learners. While many did not start out displaying these characteristics, they readily picked up on developmental efforts."

Prove your commitment

Women also have to demonstrate again and again that they are committed to work. This is partly because of assumptions about plans for family and career breaks. Assumptions are made without checking, and a break is interpreted as demonstrating a lack of commitment. This is exacerbated because the decision-makers are usually men who are more familiar with how men manage their careers (and that's the pattern that looks like "commitment" to them). An HR leader in North America told us: "Leaders in organisations need to stop looking at women from a 'cost savings' or 'expense' perspective. 'Oh geez, she's pregnant? That's gonna cost us.' And look at contributions and behaviours. How have they contributed? How have they behaved?"

Interviewees in our research also commented on how sapping it was to be constantly under scrutiny. One young woman said there was "an assumption that when I got married I would have children and therefore not be as devoted to my career, so I was passed over for a promotion – just after I came back from honeymoon!" Another commented that being asked to attend overnight workshops and conferences at short notice penalised women with childcare responsibilties and failure to attend was deemed to be a lack of flexibility and commitment.

And another women told us that, "Attitudes that women will only be useful in the short term and will not remain with the business indefinitely get in the way of moving forward."

Assumed not to have the skills

The defining female traits of being caring, warm, deferential, emotional, sensitive, and so on can be valuable, of course. But the assumption is that if someone is to be successful they must exhibit the traits previously demonstrated in the role. The result is what psychologist Madeline Heilman of New York University calls a "lack of fit" between supposed female talents and the attributes considered necessary for the job, typically masculine attributes. When managers have little information about what a candidate is *actually* like, they fill in their knowledge gap with these descriptive assumptions, often to the detriment of women.

A 2014 study by Ernesto Reuben of Columbia Business School demonstrated the consequences of this type of bias during job searches. Participants were asked to hire candidates on the basis of a mathematical task that both genders performed equally well in. The participants were twice as likely to hire the man even when the candidates were identically qualified for the simple reason that women are *seen* as being worse at maths than men.

In another study in 2005 by Madeline Heilman and Michelle Haynes participants were asked to read a description of a traditionally male role of investment portfolio management performed by a mixed male and female team. In the absence of information about individual contributions to the work, participants rated the women as having been less influential and playing minor roles. "Those negative expectations are lethal," says Heilman.

Women need to meet more rigorous criteria

Another double standard is that the criteria for promotion or hiring are applied rigorously to women and leniently to men.

Objective job-role criteria are defined with the aim of eliminating favouritism, but leniency bias occurs when the rules are rigorously applied to members of an out-group but leniently to members of an in-group. Several research studies have found that the criteria for a role are adjusted to match whatever the preferred male candidate has. In one example, several women were turned down for an academic role because they had not completed their PhD. Yet a man was appointed who had still to complete his.

Lower requirements for men

There is also evidence of the criteria for a specific job shifting to less rigorous standards for male candidates. In one study participants gave less weight to both education *and* work experience when a woman had them than when a man had them. And this tendency was stronger in those who rated themselves as unbiased.

Some researchers have tested the presence of hidden gender biases in the real world and found similar results. A research team led by psychologist Corinne Moss-Racusin sent science faculty at top universities applications for a lab manager position. The resumes were identical except for male or female names for the candidates, yet the faculty still rated the male candidates as more competent and hireable than the woman.

Be modest about those reward expectations!

In the process of hiring, the issue of salary negotiation is fraught with double standards. A joint study by Carnegie Mellon and Harvard gave participants descriptions of men and women with equivalent qualifications who had applied for a fictitious job. When told that some candidates had tried to negotiate for a higher salary, the study participants – both men and women – were twice as likely to find fault with the women who negotiated than with the men who negotiated.

Pushy women are less likely to be hired and this bias against women negotiating adds to the gender pay gap (as we described in Chapter 6).

High rewards could make the men jealous...

What's more, when a woman finally makes it to the highest echelons of the organisation, she may be given the responsibilities, but not the title, the salary and the benefits that go with it.

When co-author Jan was appointed managing director at the bank where she had worked for several years, she didn't get the benefits that went with the role for some months, ostensibly to prevent arousing antagonism amongst her peers. And a colleague of Jan's who some years ago was the first woman to qualify for a company car was told she had to have a second-hand pool car to avoid arousing jealousy amongst her male colleagues.

Penalties for women's flexible working

In the Head Heart + Brain research, many leaders told us that flexible working was an important area of focus, not least because they saw it as the way work would be designed in the future. But women still experience a penalty for asking for and working flexibly.

In a study by Christin Munsch at the University of Connecticut, the reactions that men and women received when making flexible work requests were found to be quite different – and biased in favour of men.

Munsch studied over 600 working-age individuals, all from the United States. Participants were shown a transcript of what they believed was a real conversation between an employee and a human resource officer. Unknown to the participants, Munsch modified the transcript in a few ways to alter the work arrangements, and most importantly the gender of the employee and their reason for making the request: some employees were requesting flexibility because of childcare, others for non-family reasons. All participants, regardless of transcript shown, were asked to evaluate the employee based on likability, dependability, and dedication to the job, as well as how likely they would be to accommodate the employee's request.

But not for men...

In comparing the different reactions the transcripts elicited, Munsch found that when male employees requested flexible schedules to accommodate childcare requests, almost 70% of participants were either likely or very likely to grant the request. When female employees made the same request, only around 57% said they would grant the request. In addition, participants were much more likely to evaluate the men as likable and committed than the women.

Women already experience double standards in performance evaluation, and the effect of this is amplified when they are working flexibly. A research participant said, "Work has become more flexible but our data is showing that people who work virtually get less favourable ratings because they are not physically seen." Given that more women work virtually to fit around family commitments, this is potentially another penalty they experience.

Why all this persists

"We like to think of ourselves as really fair and unbiased," says Victoria Brescoll from the Yale School of Management where she studies stereotypes and collaborated on the lab manager hiring study we've referred to. "So, when these things come out it's surprising to us. There's a certain amount of denial: 'Oh, it's not me. It doesn't happen to me.'"

Brescoll also says she suspects the biases are so well hidden in the social psyche that they're hard to spot, let alone change. After all, no one wants to think of themselves as sexist these days. And studies have found that women themselves display the same biases, often evaluating female employees less favourably than males, and expecting more of them.

One of the most common claims is that gender bias is not a problem because the organisation is a meritocracy. By which they mean people are judged based on their contribution. But studies have found that companies that espouse meritocratic values actually consider gender bias less often and display more bias than companies that don't claim to be meritocracies. Furthermore, implicit bias does not correlate with explicit bias, and everyone tends to think that their own actions are less influenced by bias than they are. The first step to overcoming our biases is to learn about them. The second step is to get help to notice when we apply them.

Career hacks

Tactics for challenging double standards

Be known: Because *prove-it-again* is a bias based on a stereotyped view of women's behaviour and abilities, the expectation is decreased when people get to know you personally (you're an engineer with deep expertise and a loud laugh, rather than the woman doing a male job).

Be known for *something*: excelling at a specialty or for a high-profile initiative is a good way to become known and acquire experience. "Dare the difference," as Christine Lagarde Managing Director of the International Monetary Fund, advises. But she says do so skilfully. Don't just do it casually; and never confuse "being authentic" with "fatal flaws" such as treating people poorly.

Be visible: Be consistent in seeking high-visibility assignments and speaking up during meetings, and find a mentor who can help make you even more visible. Show your competence by consistently performing well while also remaining true to your own values.

Own your success: Women can start to combat stereotypes by "owning" their successes and not internalising failures. Stop waiting until you satisfy every requirement to apply for a more senior role. Talk positively about your achievements, if only to yourself, and take credit for your successes.

Avoid burnout: Working hard is crucial to success, and one way of proving your competence, but it can be stressful and isolating, and can eventually affect the quality of your work. Know when you are working just to satisfy the double standard and leave some energy for yourself. Know what stresses and what relaxes you at both work and home, and leave time for rejuvenation.

Talk openly about the issue: Confront a difficult situation by openly addressing any double standards: people often make assumptions they're not aware of. Arrange with colleagues to point out when the same criteria are not being applied to men and women (it's easier than being a lone voice). Advocate for others and raise the standard of objective evaluation across the board. And if you're dealing with a bully, it's better to do it publicly so that you have witnesses and backup if needed.

Form a posse: When women promote their accomplishments they're often seen as pushy and self-promoting. So it can help to build an informal, mixed-gender group of peers, that deliberately promotes its members' accomplishments. It may sound all-American, but it's effective!

Pause for reflection: Serious issues need reflection, and many research respondents suggest it's wise to get a second opinion. Accusing someone of sexism rarely leads to productive dialogue. When dealing with someone receptive you can argue for the promotion or raise by listing your accomplishments.

Ask for your dues: If you're repeatedly given the difficult clients or passed over for the experience building projects develop a strategy to ask for what you are due - using clear and effective communication. A manager we know emphasised the importance of clarity. The best strategy, she noted, is being clear. "The first choice that I made was to be myself and to be transparent," she said.

Re-frame the situation as advantageous: One woman told us: "I don't feel that my career has been harder because I am a woman. I feel I have been given a lot of opportunity, and if I have ever been slightly disadvantaged, I've been advantaged just as many times. I think that all of our uniqueness works for us and against us at different times."

Minimise the issue: Ignoring double standards can be a way to just get things done, even if you're not changing the system. One respondent in our research described her strategy as "gender-neutral": just focusing on the relationships, and the task at hand, and her own ability rather than calling out the different criteria being applied.

Meena now realises she's been reading those micro-messages accurately, especially at meetings where she sometimes had to put men right. Yes, she's being treated differently because she's a woman: her achievements aren't being equally recognised. She's determined not to let it hold her back, even if that means going to another company to get the promotion she deserves.

Exploring further

Articles, blogs and podcasts

The Myth of the Catty Woman, Sheryl Sandberg and Adam Grant (The biggest enemy of women is a powerful woman? Statistically that isn't true.) New York Times

How female leaders should handle double standards, Herminia Ibarra, Harvard Business Review

Reasons you were not promoted that are totally unrelated to gender, Homa Mojtabai (Humorous justifications from the other side of the desk that will strike a chord with many women.) McSweeneys. net

Gender Bias Bingo (Share your experiences of gender bias for a chance to win the coveted t-shirt.) GenderBiasBingo.com

Why Some Men Pretend to Work 80 Hour Weeks, Erin Reid (Expectations of long hours and over-commitment to the job are a problem for men as well.) Harvard Business Review

Videos

How Many Micro-Inequities Can You Spot? Skill Boosters (Spot the subtle, often unconscious messages that devalue, discourage and impair workplace performance.) YouTube (1:34)

The types of micro-messages we all send in conversations, Binna Kandola (An explanation of what micro-inequities are.) YouTube (2:30)

Little Things Mean a Lot: Micro-inequities to Micro-affirmations, Learn.com (Powerful examples of influential micro-behaviours in this short video of a team meeting.) YouTube (6:02)

Some Reflections on the Dearth of Women in Science, Ben Barres (The professor of neurobiology at Stanford disagrees with his Harvard colleagues Larry Summers, Steven Pinker, and Harvey Mansfield about the supposed innately limited abilities of women in science.) Harvard University (1:48:32)

If Men Were Treated Like Women in The Office, Carly Fiorina (A brief and funny look at double standards at work.) YouTube (1:30)

14.
Resisting the backlash against strong women

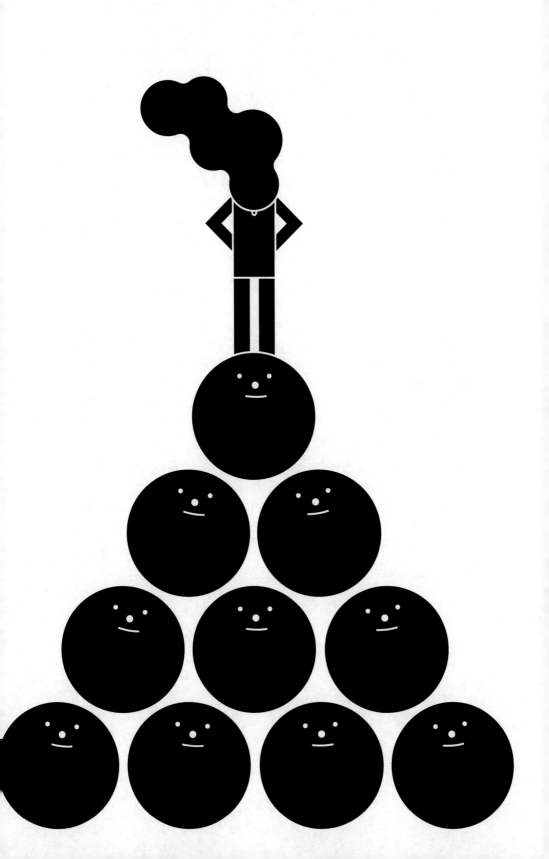

Jay has just been promoted to become the youngest business unit director in the company (next stop: the management committee). Meena is one step below him – she had to move to another division to get the promotion she needed.

Celebrations all round. Meena feels she has more chance of progression in her new division but she has been getting some feedback that she's too direct and confrontational. Does she need to be more careful about balancing competence and assertiveness with warmth, to avoid alienating "sensitive men"?

Jay tells her it isn't so much what she's doing or not doing: he's heard how some of the other directors talk about the smart women coming up through the ranks. Some of them think they're getting a bit of an easy ride, and need more time at the coalface to learn "the way things are done." Jay thinks Meena needs to find a sponsor within the organisation: someone on the management committee of the overall company who really has a stake in her success. He believes the divisional managing director he reported to performed this role for him.

More than 40 years after the Equal Pay and Sex Discrimination laws were enacted in the UK, just 10 women hold CEO positions in UK FTSE 250 companies. And according to professional boards forum BoardWatch, which tracks the appointment of women to UK FTSE 350 companies, just 6% of executive directors of FTSE 350 companies are women. That's a vanishingly small proportion of women getting the crucial experience to be on the candidate list for the CEO role when it comes up.

What accounts for this gross imbalance in power and opportunity at the heart of our economies? Why don't more women make the breakthrough to the highest positions of decision-making? Lots of theories exist, and one of them is about the strenuous efforts men (and some women) make to keep the traditional hierarchy in place.

Women's experiences

Consider your own experiences. You're in meeting with a number of your peers. The man to your left is getting agitated about the direction the meeting is going: he stands, he emphasises each point by jabbing the end of his pen on the table, and his voice gets louder and more emphatic. "Wow, Rob's just not going to let this one go," comments the person on the other side of you.

Another colleague, who vehemently disagrees, interrupts and talks over Rob, pointing at him as he makes his points in refutation. "Go, Pete!" says another person at the table: "tell it like it is." "Okay lads," interrupts the senior executive: "it's great you're so passionate about this but let's not have blood on the floor."

You disagree with the solutions both of them are proposing, which will impact badly on your team. You also stand to speak (you feel it would look less-committed if you stayed in your seat), and you speak equally forcefully. But it's not going down well. No-one's responding; their notepads suddenly seem terribly interesting. The boss interrupts with: "I think we can leave the emotion out of this," and you catch a smirk from your neighbour. As you're all leaving you hear someone remark: "She really goes over the top!"

Recognise this scenario?

Versions of this story were told to use by several of the women we interviewed for our research. They were prepared for the fact that, in order to operate in a male-dominated world, they might have to mug up on the football results each weekend (as one HR director told us). What they weren't prepared for was the active antagonism they seemed to attract the more influential they became. "Boys will be boys" seemed to be the response to assertive male behaviour, but comments about "women with sharp elbows" were made about their own tactics.

The HR director said quite clearly that she was unable to challenge many of the biased and crazy ideas the male-dominated board came up with, for fear of being ostracised. Other senior women told us they did take a stance but frequently got called names as a result. Unbelievable as it may seem in 40 years into "non-discrimination", being called a "bitch" or a "ball-breaker" were among the milder epithets.

In our research, it became clear that many women understand that they might be respected, but they wouldn't be liked. More than that: if they act assertively, they will face hostility. And research at Rutgers University in New Jersey has found the same. Women who challenge the established hierarchy suffer penalties and are ostracised and this hostile response is exacerbated when men feel threatened.

It's time for change

Women are fed up and feel it's time organisations took more decisive action to address the discrimination. One senior woman told us: "I believe this is a time for 'all hands-on deck'. When you have a burst pipe in your house, you don't keep stirring the soup. You find the buckets, you call the plumber, and you channel all your resources into fixing the problem. Gender balance is that kind of issue. We've been talking about it for long enough: now's the time to get everyone on board, and if necessary take the steps to incentivise the behaviour we want to see."

The penalties of challenging the hierarchy

When we discussed stereotypes earlier (in Chapter 2) we recognised that we're socialised to see men in senior, more powerful or highly technical roles, and women in supportive, caring and lower-status roles. We are also socialised to think men can be "aggressive and driven" about their work whilst women must be "sensitive and collaborative". And the evidence suggests that keeping this hierarchy in place is the root of many of the biased and sexist patterns that we see entrenched in organisations.

Research led by social psychologist Laurie Rudman at Rutgers University has found that women who take a strong stance challenging the established hierarchy risk social and economic penalties. Both men and women have a subconscious tendency towards this punitive response, which may be conscious or completely unconscious; Rudman called it "the backlash."

This maintenance of the social hierarchy is the basis of the bias we have discussed throughout this book, from sexist language, to women continually having to prove their value at work, to very direct ways of putting women in their place including surprisingly open scorn, derogatory language, and office sabotage.

Awareness alone doesn't change behaviour

Researchers have found that when people are alerted to stereotypes this behaviour doesn't change. Indeed, in a number of experiments by Michelle Duguid of Washington University and Melissa Thomas-Hunt of the University of Virginia, participants who were informed about the prevalence of stereotypes actually down-rated women, even when asked to try to avoid thinking in terms of stereotypes.

Why does this happen? A clue comes from social psychologist Robert Cialdini's work on stolen wood, and the use of hotel towels.

"Normalising" antisocial behaviour

Cialdini has found that making people aware, asking nicely or even instructing them how to behave has no effect, and in some cases increases the antisocial behaviour. Asking people to re-use their hotel towels, or not to souvenir wood from a petrified forest, actually increased towel use and wood theft. The message about the results of this behaviour (the energy cost of laundering towels; 6% of the forest is being lost...) in effect tells people that what is happening is common, most people do it; it's *normal.*

And "normal" is acceptable to very many people. It's when we *don't* do what everyone else does that we're "deviant," and deviant behaviour will be punished by our in-group (by anything from a raised eyebrow to gentle mockery to not being invited to important meetings). This "socially acceptable theory" explains why both women and men penalise strong women who step outside the established hierarchy and blaze new trails through corporate management.

Cialdini reworded the signage to tell forest visitors how many people *don't* take souvenirs of wood, or how many hotel guest *do* re-use their towels, and the behaviour changed. Which tells us that we need to reframe our national conversation so that women-as-leaders are "the new normal."

Stepping outside normal

Of course some women do manage to step outside the stereotype and be the trailblazers. For them, other values were more important than "fitting in". You could say their socialisation was faulty, like the girl who was taught she was just as good as a boy, or the girl who takes discouragement as a challenge.

Tanja Wielgoss, a partner at management consultants A.T. Kearney in Dusseldorf, writes in a story for Sheryl Sandberg's Leanin.org: "I can still vividly recall our new 10th grade math teacher coming into the classroom, taking a look round and pronouncing: 'No need to worry if you girls find things a bit difficult – it's only natural.' That was my first 'Lean in' moment. I vowed to do at least as well as the best boy in the class. And I did."

How to stand up to the onslaught...

Evidence tells us that direct confrontation and "calling out" biased behaviour as it occurs is often ineffective. We can recognise now what triggers the defensive bluster and denial on the part of the person responsible (their need to follow group behaviour is more important than the risk of upsetting a "deviant," outspoken woman).

Studies by social psychologists Melissa Williams from Emory University and Larissa Tiedens from Stanford set out to test the hypothesis that a response which doesn't directly challenge stereotypical gender roles and offend the social order might go "unpunished" (that is to say, be effective without creating even more antagonism).

Explicit behaviour is penalised

Williams and Tiedens carried out a meta-analysis of existing research and found, unsurprisingly, that women were liked less, by both men and women, when they acted assertively. However, when they split the studies into the type of dominant behaviour measured, they found some interesting results.

Explicit behaviour, including making demands and arguing in favour of a course of action (as with "calling out," above) was disliked, and both men and women "penalised" the behaviour when it occurred (including saying they would be less likely to hire that person). And women were disliked more for the behaviour (that's the backlash at work).

But *implicit* behaviour, or "implicit dominance" – including nonverbal cues such as expansive posture, standing close to the other person and speaking without hesitation – had no effect on likability.

Challenging bias without triggering a backlash

The conclusion by Williams and Tiedens: avoid outright demands and instead respond to a biased put-down by showing dominance through body language. Use bold gestures, speak without hesitation, look people directly in the eye and lean in.

It may seem odd that people wouldn't notice a woman's bold body language and recognise it as challenging the stereotype. But according to Williams and Tiedens, body language is often subtle enough that we process it unconsciously. It would take focused attention to deconstruct it in a way that can be contrasted with expectations: "Hmmm... that pose means power, and women shouldn't be powerful, so that feels wrong..." The researchers draw a parallel with findings on "priming" (see Chapter 7 in the other half of this book): signals to the brain in words, images or other cues that operate below the radar.

Taking the opportunity to speak, speaking more clearly and making eye contact when speaking all signal competence and leadership, and can be used to signal power and get your point across without triggering an antagonistic response.

Become fluent in body language

Deborah Gruenfeld, of Stanford's graduate school of business, argues that all groups require some kind of hierarchy, and women have to learn how to operate cleverly within a hierarchy if they want to be successful. And she too believes the most effective impact is made through behaviour and non-verbal cues.

When we want to make an impression, most of us think about what we want to say. Gruenfeld says we should pay more attention to body language: words account for just 7% of what our audience will process and take away, while body language, voice tone and voice pace account for the rest.

This non-verbal communication is so effective because we have a specific area of the brain for reading and understanding people's meaning and intentions: the medial prefrontal cortex – part of the default system – because it's the activity we default to whenever we are not undertaking a specific task. We automatically read body language all the time, so Gruenfeld recommends that this is a language women should become fluent in.

A new body language: playing high or low

Gruenfeld says we have two main ways of interacting with others within a hierarchy, which she calls "playing high" and "playing low". (For examples see Keith Johnston's book, and actors demonstrating the techniques, in *Exploring further* at the end of this chapter and Chapter 11 *Career hacks* for a list of high and low behaviours.)

Playing high is about creating psychological distance between you and the other person, and establishing a sense of authority over them:

- Lean back
- Keep your head still
- Show very little or no reaction to other people's comments
- Speak at a slower pace in full sentences
- Make eye contact for longer than usual with the person you're talking to
- Make expansive gestures

Playing low is about creating psychological closeness between you and the other person, and making them feel that you're approachable (watch Woody Allen in any of his movies):

> • Take up less space: fold yourself in, crouch down to their level, point your toes inward
> • Use body-protective gestures: fold your arms across your body, cross your legs, touch your face
> • Avoid eye contact, except briefly just to check in
> • Pitch your voice higher
> • Speak in short sentences that are more like fragments
> • Speak with obvious emotion in your tone

Understanding how to act with power

The tendency when first learning these techniques is to avoid doing anything on the playing low list and try to play high all the time. But any teacher, or group-leader, will tell you that this is a mistake. Sometimes you create the most powerful impact by being quiet, and bringing a room to silence by example. And lowering your energy to match your audience's, before raising it to the level you want them to experience is the kind of control only a truly confident leader achieves.

And some people try to play both high and low at the same time, creating a confusing image that doesn't achieve its intended purpose.

You need to work out what will achieve the best result with a specific person, or circumstance, to achieve the outcome you want. We get into the habit of playing the same way with the same people, for example, playing low with the boss you worked for early in your career, even though you are now peers. Or playing high with someone you were at one time competing with, even though it would now be useful to be allies on a project.

Know when to play high or low

Just as you choose the appropriate clothes for an important meeting, this is a behaviour you can make a choice about:

> • Play high when you need to reinforce your actual authority, when authoritativeness is called for, or when your status is ambiguous in a competitive environment.
> • Play low when you want to build personal connection, when the energy in the room is low and you need to get

people to open up to you, and when you need to make other people feel important.

Let's take an example. A senior woman may come into a meeting with the new graduate intake playing high: she is introduced with her corporate title and credentials. She can then build trust by playing low: not taking up too much space, being warm, inviting questions, telling the story of how terrified she was on her first day as a graduate. A little later, when she needs to make a strong case for something important like integrity, or working hard, she can play high and it will feel less cold and more like a legitimate show of authority.

In the end, being able to play high and low when it's called for are signals that represent real authority and power. So, it's important that if you play high you can back it up with competence (you are the expert in the room on the client account). It's important to recognise how your behaviour can influence how others treat you. But real authority and status come from consistently doing things that are good for "the group", so remember to focus on that too.

The evidence shows that being able to manage your behaviour in this way gets you the results you want without triggering a defensive response: an altogether more productive way of undermining the stereotype.

Career hacks

Knowing how confidence feels

Posture can change not only how others perceive us, but how we perceive ourselves – creating the kind of confidence that's impregnable to a hostile response.

Expansive postures *create* confidence

You don't believe it? Try these two quick exercises linked to Harvard social psychologist Amy Cuddy's research:

> **Exercise 1:** Sit in a "constricted pose": hunch over, touch your knees together, put your hands between your legs, lower your head and look down. Hold that position for 30 seconds and then say out loud: *"I am invincible. I'm totally in charge. I'm on top of the world."* Are you sounding believable?

> **Exercise 2:** Sit in a "power pose": spread your legs wide in your chair, puff your chest out, take up lots of space. Drape your arm along the chair next to you, cross your legs with your ankle up on your opposite knee. After holding this pose for 30 seconds, say out loud: *"I am totally weak and helpless. I am nothing. I am worthless"*. Is it all-but-impossible for you to sound convincing?

Tweak your tone and posture

This is an exercise Jan uses in Head Heart + Brain's leadership programmes, which has amazing results (you'll need the assistance of an observer/coach). First of all, pick a specific meeting or presentation which you have coming up: you're going to rehearse just your introduction, or the critical message you want to get across.

Don't worry too much about what you say; focus on your body posture, your tone of voice, your energy and how fast you're speaking. Your observer will watch you do one short run-through of no longer than 30 seconds or a minute. Your coach then suggests one small adjustment in one dimension (of posture, tone, speed or energy). Repeat the rehearsal with that improvement. Keep making small adjustments, one at a time, to just one of the dimensions, until your observer thinks you're achieving the best possible impact, and you feel confident.

Getting the introduction of your meeting or presentation right sets you up for success for the rest. You are in the right state of mind and body and your audience will start with the best possible impression which predisposes them to continue to see you positively.

And it works...

People are always surprised at how much difference these small changes make and how successful they are when they put them into practice. One particularly sceptical leader needed to attend a meeting with his CEO in the middle of a workshop with us (he was presenting a radical new approach which could have an uncertain reception). He rehearsed his meeting in the exercise. When he returned from the actual encounter with the CEO he was beaming: he'd put the coaching into practice and the pitch went flawlessly. Proposal accepted. He was a lot less sceptical about the rest of the workshop content, and so were his colleagues.

Learn to power pose

Amy Cuddy has found that adopting a power posture for around two minutes can change self-perception and our perception of other people.

When you need to be confident, and want others to think you are, spend a few minutes in a power pose. It sounds silly, but stand like Superwoman: legs wide and hands on hips (you could make this the position you adopt while you review your presentation notes). Or sit back with your hands behind your head and your feet up on the desk. Or be the champion who's crossed the finishing line first in the hundred metres: the idea is to get comfortable with expansive body language.

Power posing prior to an important meeting ensures you go in feeling you have the power to bring your full self to the situation, without any of the misgivings or inhibitions that might usually hold you back. This allows you not just to be stronger, but also to be more open and trusting. In the meeting, be sure to display some balance. Use strong, open body posture, don't slouch and be as big as you comfortably can be but remember also to smile, make one-to-one connections and invite people into the conversation.

Meena has signed up to work with a coach on how she uses her body language to project authority without triggering hostility. The techniques have been a revelation to her and she has been surprised to find how much more confident she actually feels. "I wish I'd learned about this years ago: it would have helped me!"

She's taken Jay's advice about actively seeking a sponsor. Her division managing director and the head of HR have both agreed they will help her set up a meeting with the overall company CEO to promote the idea of introducing sponsors for senior women across the organisation. (The head of HR says the CEO finally "saw the light" on gender in the workplace when his daughter left university and told him about the gender bias she was experiencing at work. He's now looking to do more to promote equality.) Meena's goal is to get him to sponsor her!

Exploring further

Books

Playing Big: Practical Wisdom for Women Who Want to Speak Up, Create and Lead, Tara Mohr

Impro (Performance Books): Improvisation and the Theatre, Keith Johnstone (A hundred practical techniques for encouraging spontaneity and originality by catching the subconscious unawares.)

Articles, blogs and podcasts

Why Are There So Few Women in the C-Suite? Matt Palmquist (A new study finds that despite progress on gender equity, there seems to be an implicit quota on women holding senior positions at large companies.) Strategy+Business blogs

How Women Can Lean in Without Backlash, Matthew Hutson (How women can show dominance through body language while avoiding outright demands.)

Videos and webinars

Power and Influence, Deborah Gruenfeld (Becoming fluent in matching body language to each situation can be a source of power and influence.) YouTube (20:51)

Your Body Language Shapes Who You Are, Amy Cuddy (How "power posing" can affect testosterone and cortisol levels in the brain, and might have an impact on success.) TED.com (20:55)

Status Exercise, Improv Book (Some easy actors' improvisation techniques that express status.) YouTube (3:04)

Charisma, Leadership and the Imposter Syndrome, Olivia Fox Cabane (A summary of her book.) YouTube (27:37)

Playing Big: Find Your Voice, Your Mission, Your Message, Tara Mohr. (Great tools and strategies to help women project a more commanding image.) YouTube (29:21)

The Differences of Playing High and Low, Dan Klein and Melissa Briggs. (Stanford lecturer and acting coach take turns at playing high and low status during a mock interview.) YouTube (2:21)

15.
Leaders breaking free of the stereotypes

It's time to break out the champagne. There's been a major restructuring at Multinational Trading: a lot of the "dead wood" have been asked to leave and Jay and Meena have both been promoted to the management committee. They're each heading a division of the organisation as managing directors. Meena's sponsor really came through for her and his belated commitment to a better gender balance has worked in her favour.

Jay and Meena now need to consider how they can develop and promote the kind of leaders they believe will drive the right results and culture in the organisation. Starting with how leadership is defined.

It's been a tough route to the top for Meena. Like many other women she's had to battle against prejudice, with people doubting all along the way whether she had what it takes. She hasn't benefitted from a groundswell of female peer support; nor, sadly, does she represent an exciting new wave of women corporate leaders.

The great change isn't happening yet

Her appointment comes at a time when research by Pipeline recruitment consultancy in the UK found there had been *no* progress on the number of women on FTSE 350 companies' executive committees over the previous year, and women accounted for only 16% of the appointments in 2016. At least Meena will be one more positive statistic, but progress is depressingly slow.

And on company boards, the next step for Meena, the number of women being newly appointed is slowing: only 29% of new appointments in the UK in 2016, *down* from just over 30% in previous years. This compares unfavourably with Western Europe where 35% of board appointments were women; in the US, board diversity has stagnated as well, with women making up only a fifth of boards, a growth of just a miniscule 1% since 2012.

The stereotyped model of leadership

The world Jay and Meena are entering is overwhelmingly, and stereotypically, male. And that can work against modern men like Jay as much as for women: a study by Stephanie Johnson from Colorado State University showed that men who don't conform to the aggressive male stereotype receive lower evaluations as leaders, just as women do. (The study found women need to be both sensitive and strong as leaders, while men were just required to be strong.)

For Meena, research by Catalyst, the non-profit promoting equality in the workplace, indicates that "No matter how women choose to lead, they are perceived as 'never just right...' If women business leaders act consistently with gender stereotypes, they are considered too soft. If they go against gender stereotypes, they are considered too tough."

Jayne-Anne Gadhia, head of Virgin Money, tells a story about how she was once told by a boss that he'd turned her down for a promotion because she didn't have a thick-enough skin or the ability to bullshit. Twenty-five years later, at the top of the UK banking sector, she says: "I hope I haven't got a thick skin and don't bullshit. I do think the culture that required [those characteristics] has changed."

Self-perpetuating promotion criteria

A report by Annika Warren from Drexel University for Catalyst describes a vicious cycle with senior male leaders favouring promotion criteria that reflect their own experience (consistent with the brain's certainty bias), and HR professionals implementing their wishes instead of challenging them. And this experience is happening in Europe too. One of our 26 year-old female survey respondents from Eastern Europe told us that in her organisation: "There is a promotion bias towards males... most senior members of the firm are male and [this] limits the ability to have a champion or mentor who can fight for opportunities [for you]."

In the Catalyst research the top three characteristics chosen by HR talent managers to evaluate their senior executives were: results-driven, action-oriented and problem-solving. But Meena and Jay represent a new breed of thoughtful, reflective leaders who are more likely to be selected by different criteria such as being collaborative, mindful of others and skilled at building cohesive teams. They have made it to the highest echelons almost despite their particular skills and qualities, but are now in a position to support and accelerate the structural changes which will make organisations more diverse and more inclusive, attracting the best people while maximising the performance and innovation.

And for leaders on the way up a chink of hope comes from a meta-analysis by Northwestern University which shows that there is a slight shift towards a more androgynous view of management, at least for lower-level leadership positions and in educational institutions.

How men and women approach leadership differently

Management Research Group (MRG) has been studying gender and leadership since 1998. Looking at behaviours and competencies in 13,100 leaders from more than 15 countries they have found that women place more emphasis on three clusters of skills or abilities:

- Behaviours that support transparency and connection: including enthusiasm, feedback, communication, and empathy.
- Accountability and results: including goal attainment, leadership responsibility and the willingness to be forceful.
- Execution: being organised, attending to details, and following up to ensure implementation is on track.

By contrast, men believe leadership is about:

- Thinking strategically: contemplating both conservative and innovative options, and acting independently.
- Being cooperative, asking for assistance, and delegating to others.
- Persuading others to endorse their ideas and proposals.

These are all important leadership competencies, and it's clear that any leadership team will be stronger if it embraces all of them. But men's and women's priorities *are* different, and if the frameworks to identify and select future leaders are defined by men then women will continue to fail to meet the criteria.

Comparing men and women as leaders

But which "brand" of leader is most effective? When you look at the hard data it's hard to understand why men continue to dominate leadership when women actually out-perform them.

Assessed for competency by their bosses, their peers and their direct reports, women were rated higher than men on twelve out of the twenty-two skills measured by MRG. Including various forms of interpersonal effectiveness and credibility, *and* the two overarching leadership skills: overall effectiveness and future potential.

Men scored equally with women on seven and were rated higher-than women on just three leadership competencies: business aptitude, financial understanding, and ability to see the big picture. (Note: the criteria for promotion commonly cover many skills, but these are usually set as the *key* determinants for promotion.)

Shout it from the rooftops: women are more effective leaders!

Not convinced? Let's look at a larger data set. Leadership development consultancy Zenger Folkman collects 360° feedback from leading organisations worldwide; analysis of a sample of just under 16,000 leaders (two-thirds male, one-third female) found that women were rated at 54% on overall effectiveness, compared with 51% of men. (A 2% advantage may not seem impressive, but on a sample of this size it is statistically significant.)

Zenger Folkman's studies have found that there are different ratings of leadership effectiveness at different career stages. There is very little perceived difference in leadership ability between women and men at the start of their careers: men are seen to be very slightly more effective than women but the difference is small. But as women mature they are judged to be more effective overall and also more effective than their male colleagues. Women's lead continues to widen until they reach their 60s when they're nine percentile points ahead of men, at which point men begin to catch up.

This is powerful evidence of how stereotypes override evidence of actual effectiveness: the media and myths override the facts. Women take heart: not only *can* you do it, you *are* doing it.

Women keep improving

Not only do women out-perform men as leaders overall but according to Bob Sherwin, COO of Zenger Folkman, their significant improvement after the age of 40 can be attributed to their achievements in a competency called "Practicing Self Development". This is a measure of the extent to which people ask for feedback and make changes based upon it: men get worse at doing this as they get older.

All of this data tells us that women do have skills, or develop the skills, that are more effective in leadership (collaboration, trust, empathy...) but can also hold people to account and achieve results. This is a brain-savvy leader (see Chapter 15 in the other book). These abilities are not innate: we know from studies on the male and female brain that there is no significant difference in biological development to explain these behavioural differences. These abilities have developed on the job (or, rather, in life.) The challenge now is for women to get recognition for them.

We need fewer heroes...

One way to change ideas of what good leadership looks like is to pay more attention to what is actually *effective* rather than what has been expected. Sacha Romanovitch, the first woman CEO of accounting and consulting company Grant Thornton UK, says "Established notions of leadership are letting women down. The 'hero model' of leadership, where the individual commanding must be perfect and the job all-consuming, is still extremely prevalent, whilst more collaborative and inclusive forms of leadership are overlooked."

How to encourage the new kind of leader

So how can we untangle leadership from this heroic masculine model? According to one study cited by Catalyst, something as simple as changing the language about leadership activities can have a dramatic effect. Leaders described less as driven and assertive and more as collaborative and mindful. One of our survey participants, in a government department told us, "One [of our] recent job adverts read like something out of boy's own adventures. When pointed out to the manager, he was genuinely shocked as he hadn't read it that way and genuinely wanted to recruit some women into technical roles and had been puzzled they weren't applying"

Another study found that personal exposure to counter-stereotypes – male midwives, or female mechanics – alters the way we form our world view and process social information. Of course, it would be much better if this happened early in childhood, but it is never too late to start to erode stereotypes and open the door to more inclusivity.

There's evidence to show (cited in Chapter 2 of this half of the book on stereotypes) that careful decision-making, where people slow down and reflect on their judgements, can help to reduce biased evaluations of women in leadership positions. And anti-bias education amongst university professors has been shown to improve the environment in their departments.

Reviewing and redesigning recruitment helps to bring more women into previously male-dominated roles, and similar approaches can be used for internal promotions as well.

But the most powerful re-writing of leadership will come from having more women in leadership roles, exercising power in new ways that may involve less fanfare and no satin capes.

Career hacks

Changing the organisation

Not all the female leaders interviewed for the Head Heart + Brain survey proposed radical or continual change. We can't fight wars all the time: it's too exhausting, and alienates the people we most need to influence (the men currently in power). However, we can pick our battles, pace the change and push when we need to:

In-flight change: This is a term some organisations use to describe major changes being rolled out without interrupting operations. The term has relevance for women leaders as well, in terms of meeting your targets whilst also shifting perceptions and expectations of how you perform your role.

Honour history: What got you to your leadership position may have been hard to take, but you did get here. Equally, whatever has made the organisation you work for successful means something was done right. Any conversation about the future needs to honour the past and take account of what to preserve. Not only does this protect the reputation of those who were part of the history (who may be sitting next to you in the boardroom) it also adds a degree of certainty that change is steeped in something familiar.

Make links for people: The story of any business is not a smooth upwards trajectory: all businesses have setbacks and war stories about challenges. Give the people who weathered those changes credit for what they created, and use their stories to galvanise change for the future. Find the threads that tie those past issues to the future you want to create. Remind people they've done this before, and they will know how to do it again.

Pace the change: In any major change, there will be passionate advocates who want to rush things through, overturn everything, and do away with anyone who has been a doubter. What is often *not* managed in a revolution is the aftermath (and goodness knows we've seen plenty of examples of that in recent times). Putting passions to productive use often gets better long-term results. The clever video *How to start a movement* (in *Exploring further* below) illustrates how important it is to get others on board with your cause. The people who first follow you need to be encouraged, honoured and celebrated.

Pace the change for those who aren't yet ready. Not everyone needs to come on board at the same time. Don't waste your energy or credibility on the last few doubters. As the video illustrates there will be a tipping point when it's harder to be against than to be for: that's the point you're aiming for. One of our survey participants, a 56 year-old working in the not-for-profit sector, told us: "Back in the 1990s we established a culture of promoting women into senior roles and this is now self-perpetuating."

Changing Yourself

Throughout both halves of this book we have given you tips, tools and ideas to use in your career. Here is a summary of our advice:

Develop your purpose: Unless you know *why* you want to do what you're doing, you'll become lost and unsure in the tough times. No one else is going to build the life you want, you have to do it yourself. Take the time to define your purpose, review it regularly and be proud to state it. Let your purpose guide your decisions, clarify conflicts and help you stay motivated.

See yourself as a success: What does it look and feel like when you're successful? What are people saying, what do you say to yourself? Having a clear mental picture helps your brain to form the neuro connections which mean you feel authentic acting as a success, you are more confident and you quickly overcome that uncomfortable sense that this isn't "you".

Resilience and growth: The more you stretch outside your comfort zone the more resilience you develop. It will be hard at first but we humans are driven to explore: it gets the adrenalin and dopamine flowing. Ask yourself, "What's the stretch action here?" Your fears and a tough inner critic will pop into your head. That's normal: it's just a gremlin, created to keep you safe but which has now overstayed its welcome. Give it a name and tell it you're now moving forward.

Toughen up: Sometimes risks pay off and sometimes they don't. The trick is to know when to move on, be compassionate with yourself and learn from the experience for next time. Can you think of any leader or innovator you admire who doesn't have harsh critics as well as enthusiastic fans? Get used to wins and losses, praise and criticism, getting noticed and being ignored.

Own the label: One of the Head Heart + Brain research participants said that when she owned up to being tough, ambitious or over-demanding she dissipated criticism from other people: her colleagues could acknowledge these traits in her without the sting. Sometimes it pays to be less careful and more who you really are inside.

Act when you're *nearly* ready: There's a voice which says "You're not ready yet." It may be yours or it may be the voice of your unsupportive boss. Because you have such high standards, you can see every way that you could be more qualified, you could test one more idea. You notice every part of your plan that isn't perfect yet. But while you're sitting on your ideas and gathering more experience, the boys are getting promotions, being anointed industry visionaries, and seeing their ideas come to life in the world. They are no more ready than you, and are quite probably less-prepared. Jump in. Develop in flight.

Praise yourself: When co-author Jan first got divorced someone remarked "Well, that's the end of your jewellery collection." What she meant was: only men buy jewellery for women. You won't be surprised to hear that Jan went straight out and bought the biggest diamond she could afford. Don't wait to be praised, anointed or validated. Don't wait for someone to give you permission to lead. No one is going to discover you. (Well, actually, they will, but only after you've stepped boldly into leadership and started sharing your voice and buying your own jewels.)

Pick and choose who you listen to: Feedback is meant to be a gift but sometimes it's poison. Most brilliant women are modest (sometimes too modest): we want to gather feedback and advice. But recognise that some people won't understand what you're doing or believe that you should be doing it. Some people will find it threatening if you're challenging the hierarchy. Some people will only take on board the parts of your ideas that suit their plan. So interpret the feedback you get carefully: it's not all equally valuable. Test the advice you're given, pick out the gifts from the poison.

Risk, rest, relax: We have a special part of our system which joins the brain and the gut called the vagus nerve. Its role is to aid digestion, rest and relaxation, and is also an essential part of our immune system, promoting health and resilience. If you start doing the things that stretch you, working outside your comfort zone and being bolder, you must also regularly do things that feel safe, cosy and restorative. Vent to friends when you need to, and take a break regularly to recover and restore.

Share the brilliance: Think about how you wish you were treated. Remember when someone told you that you're great, how you were supported when you were down and when you were encouraged to take a risk. Do that for other women, and a few men. Let them know what kind of brilliance you see, and why it's so special. Call them into action. Tell them they're ready and able. Watch out for that mean thought that you had to struggle so why shouldn't they. If you're willing to help others you gain from a brain based reward which will be greater than the time and effort you may think it will take.

Be a "new" leader: By this we mean you can change things by directly fighting or by stealth. Many women told us you gain more by being the acceptable side of change: create a distinct style, be tough and sensitive, demanding and supportive, ambitious and collaborative. A new type of brain-savvy leader.

There are going to be major challenges and setbacks in their new roles, but both Jay and Meena feel they are well set up to meet them, provided they keep learning.

Jay is keen to see less "macho muscle" being exercised throughout the organisation, and more collaboration. Meena doesn't want to be seen solely as an advocate for women, but she has been inspired by women CEOs who have been powerful and visible advocates for a different style of leadership and more gender balance and diversity throughout organisations.

Exploring further

Articles, blogs and podcasts

Women and the Labyrinth of Leadership, Alice Eagly and Linda Carli (The reasons for the scarcity of women in top leadership have been misread, so the solutions that managers are investing in are not making enough of a difference.) Harvard Business Review

How Women Leaders Have Transformed Leadership, Sally Helgesen (The new model: emergent, non-positional, more inclusive and leading from the centre.) Strategy+Business blogs

How to be a more inclusive leader, Laura Swiszczowski (Research shows that inclusive leadership can drive productivity, loyalty and motivation, yet many companies fail to embrace it.) The Guardian

Inclusive Leadership: From Pioneer to Mainstream, Opportunity Now and Shapiro Consulting (What makes a great inclusive leader, how does this add value to an organisation, and how are inclusive leaders grown and developed? With self-assessment questions.) Business In the Community

The Six Signature Traits of an Inclusive Leader, Juliet Bourke, Bernadette Dillon (Diversity of markets, customers, ideas, and talent are driving the need for leaders who not only embrace individual differences, but can leverage them for competitive advantage. Also has a short video and podcast) deloitte.com

High Achieving Women Have These Six Personality Traits. Do You? Josephine Fairley, (According to a study, women business leaders share many of the same characteristics, including a healthy resiliance to anxiety. Josephine Fairley offers her relaxation tips to ensure you're not too stressed for success) The Telegraph

The Entry Level Health Care Jobs Men Are (and Are Not) Taking, Janette Dill, (As employment options shrink in parts of the Midwest, many men who once worked in manufacturing are finding new careers in health care.) Harvard Business Review.

Do Women Make Bolder Leaders than Men? Jack Zenger and Joseph Folkman, (summary of the research mentioned above) Harvard Business Review

Just About Managing: Men and Women Through the Executive Pipeline, 30% Club (Insights for people-managers on the gender diversity challenge.) 30percentclub.org

Videos and webinars

Aspire to lead, PwC (Conversations on the topics of transitioning to the workplace, building confidence and trust as a leader, and how to support gender equality in the workplace, for students and professionals.) pwc.co.uk (3:25)

Why we have too few women leaders, Sheryl Sandberg (The Facebook COO looks at why a smaller percentage of women than men reach the top of their professions, and offers three powerful pieces of advice to women.) TED.com (14:58)

How to start a movement, Derek Sivers (Music entrepreneur Sivers explains how movements really get started, with help from some surprising footage.) TED.com (5:51)

16.
Creating a gender-savvy organisation

Now that Meena and Jay are on the management committee of Multinational Trading they are in a position to influence diversity and gender policies within the organisation. They made a presentation to the board, and have now been asked to jointly lead a project to look at improving gender equality in the company. They also want to use some of the ideas they have been applying to their own teams as they have progressed through the organisation.

But they're aware that many very worthy proposals come to nothing: they want to understand what will be most effective in helping them to bring about change.

As part of the research for this book we interviewed many business and public service organisation leaders, including board and company directors, HR directors, heads of diversity and inclusion, and senior women who have made their way up through organisations and are trying to improve the balance of men and women in senior roles.

In addition, we carried out a survey in which over 1,000 men and women told us about their experiences at work. (We refer to the results throughout this book.)

Finding the lighthouse organisations

We analysed the results of our research to understand what makes the *biggest* difference in transforming organisations into more gender diverse workplaces, and used these to build our model of the success factors for a Gender-Savvy Organisation.

In any sector, there are organisations that consistently perform outstandingly well in a particular area of what they do. They are the exemplars – the lighthouse organisations. In gender equality, these are the organisations which recognise that providing opportunities for everyone, men and women, is good for business, maximises profit and serves customers and clients.

Research by Head Heart + Brain, and others, has shown that what makes them successful is usually the purpose and beliefs they apply to what they do; these in turn drive a mind-set and develop the skills which cement the success in place, providing a consistency in approach, which in turn reinforces the beliefs.

Discovering the success factors

We interviewed senior leaders in lighthouse organisations; these were the people who deeply understand why and how their organisation is executing their gender strategy so effectively. We also asked individuals about their experiences: what initiatives had helped their careers and which company policies had held them back. The in-depth interviews followed a structured format to draw out information about the initiatives that have been exceptionally successful, and the programmes that have been less successful.

Typically, we found there are a small number of patterns or sets of beliefs that make the difference. We call these the "differences that make the difference:" the success factors.

From the data, we developed a model that clearly describes the attributes and also the tensions that must be managed: what supports and what hinders success. The model provides a helpful way of describing the success factors in a common language, and pointing to the examples of excellence that we found. We also look at other research, both academic and from consulting firms, which verifies our findings or challenges them, and share that here.

Decision-makers can compare the similarities and differences between the gender equality initiatives in their own organisations and the practices in the success model: they can use it to "audit" their own practices and to identify where they need to do things differently.

The essential differences of gender-savvy organisations

When we looked for what made organisations' gender programmes successful we found four elements that made the biggest difference. No one company did all of them to the same level. Several exhibited a number of them, at different levels of maturity and confidence. Some organisations were in the early days with some elements but were confident they would make a difference, and others could point to clear evidence that a success factor had made an impact.

This model is a way of looking at where you should focus, what might be missing from your efforts, what you may be doing that is wasted effort, and tweaks you can make to how you're approaching your policy and practice.

Below, we discuss the 4 key elements of the success profile model, what they mean in practice, the science that supports them and what gets in the way. In the next chapter you'll see how you can implement change initiatives successfully, and how insights from neuroscience can help you to select or implement the parts of the model you need.

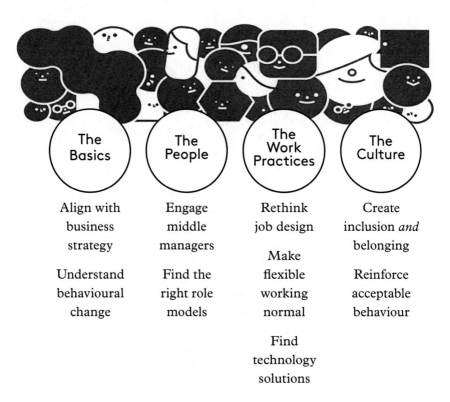

The Basics	The People	The Work Practices	The Culture
Align with business strategy	Engage middle managers	Rethink job design	Create inclusion *and* belonging
Understand behavioural change	Find the right role models	Make flexible working normal	Reinforce acceptable behaviour
		Find technology solutions	

1 The basics

Align with the business strategy

Everyone will tell you they do this but a few questions reveal that the links are often in the minds of the senior leaders rather than the people in the heart of the organisation.

The best companies could describe in some detail how initiatives helped deliver the business strategy and why they were essential to its successful implementation. So, for example, an Australian consulting firm told us a diverse workforce meant they mirrored their clients, and they could track how the different perspectives brought by women led to better solutions (for the business, and for client issues). Being more inclusive encouraged innovation and agility and reflected how they were helping clients. In short, their diversity and inclusion strategy helped them achieve their business strategy which was all about innovation and agility.

Mirroring the business strategy is also a useful tactic to ensure the programme is embedded. For example, if the business strategy has three years to run so too will the diversity and inclusion strategy.

Understanding behavioural change

The other area which was proving successful in gender projects was using an understanding of neuroscience and behavioural economics (you can also learn more about how these ideas work in the following chapter on implementation).

By far the greatest application was in unconscious bias training and many people told us this would solve their organisation's issues on bias. There was little understanding that awareness on its own would change nothing. Sadly, there seemed to be a widespread perception of "we provided this: job done."

The more insightful use of neuroscience was directed towards understanding what creates a sense of inclusion and belonging and how stereotypes could be managed. We believe there is a lot more that could be done in this area, especially in designing practice and policy to change or nudge behaviour.

Some companies we talked to were beginning to use the ideas from Iris Bohnet's book *What Works: Gender Equality By Design*, which recommends designing work practices to achieve the desired be-haviour. Head Heart + Brain has been using the same approach in redesigning performance management and training strategies, and the UK government has used these strategies to improve outcomes in a wide range of areas from health to tax collection.

2. The people

According to our research participants, middle managers make or break a gender initiative. As one senior woman said: "If your manager isn't aware of and interested in the challenges and the nuances of gender stereotypes, it's better to move on to another department or company."

A survey of leading European companies by McKinsey in 2012 suggested that while most CEOs supported moves toward gender parity, only 13% of middle managers agreed with the idea. McKinsey estimate around 70% of middle managers are men; getting them on board is the difference between real progress and platitudes.

The position of middle managers in the middle of the hierarchy means that they translate the strategic direction out to their immediate environment; the aim of gender parity espoused by a CEO is made real by middle managers changing their daily interactions around gender.

How to engage middle managers

We found that the most progressive organisations engage middle managers in understanding why gender diversity is good for them, not just good for women. Several companies gave managers targets which are part of their performance and reward evaluations, and they skilled up managers (not just senior leaders) to be inclusive, seeing their role as creating the right culture for their whole team.

There was a general belief that quotas did not work. One Australian banker said their focus on targets had backfired, with managers "gaming the numbers and promoting women before they were ready." They had also experienced men in the organisation reacting to what they perceived as unfair promotions of women. The bank has now largely dropped the "numbers game" and is instead focusing on culture change and inclusion via middle managers.

As gender advocates, middle managers need training in the subtleties micro-messages. Many of them struggle to even be aware of the signals they give to women that tell them they are valued, or that they don't belong. (We discuss the impact of these micro-messages earlier in this half of the book, in Chapter 13, and in the chapter on inclusive leadership in the other half of the book, Chapter 15.) They also set the tone for the team and how inclusive it feels; they're the people who allow (or put paid to) sexist comments and undermining behaviour like mansplaining and maninterrupting, as well as assigning the high-profile clients and projects.

Research by Elisabeth Kelan at Cranfield School of Management found four ways in which middle managers can advance the strategy:

1. Celebrating and encouraging women
2. Calling out bias
3. Championing and defending gender initiatives
4. Championing work practices such as flexible work arrangements

Managers who are focused on creating a more gender-equal work environment know how they can ensure everyone has the opportunity to contribute, and that their contribution is acknowledged, and in this way are essential contributors to the strategy on gender. Focusing on them accelerates change.

Finding the right role models

Much of the media coverage of gender at work focuses on numbers: pay inequality, and the disproportionate number of men in positions of power. But in the workplace our research participants looked for role models: women who might help them to think about what was possible, who had experience that would help them manage their careers, and who would inspire them.

There was a recognition that we need the right role models for different stages of our careers. To reduce the equality gap in leadership, intuitively it makes sense that organisations need more female leaders as role models for younger women. Certainly, our research participants frequently mentioned how it helped women to think about what is possible. One respondent who described herself as a seasoned manager said that what was needed was to "break the stereotypes: profile role models at different levels of your organisation."

Too distant is unachievable

And research also suggests that the more familiar people are with influential women in roles which are untypical, the more the stereotypes start to erode. However, research has shown that there are important subtleties to understand. If role models are *too* senior ("We've got Sheryl Sandberg / Karren Brady coming to speak!") women can devalue their own worth by comparison.

A Harvard study by Crystal Hoyt and Stefanie Simon examined the impact of female role models on women's self-perceptions and leadership aspirations during a leadership task. Being exposed to very senior successful female role models had a counterintuitively negative effect on younger women's responses to leadership situations: they became less confident and less motivated. They identified more closely with role models who weren't so remote, considering their success as attainable.

Inspiration and familiarity

Younger women may be inspired but can't always identify with a woman at the top of the organisation: the gap is too great. We need role models who are close enough to our own experience that we can identify the steps to get to where they are: how to get there from here. Or we need to have enough contact with them that it's possible to deeply understand them, not just look at them from afar.

One mechanism we know works is to provide question and answer sessions with role models who are one to two levels above. Asking the women to talk candidly about the challenges they have faced and the tactics they used, including how they managed career and family, is very effective (many men find these sessions helpful too: those committed to a 50/50 split of their own family responsibilities report that they find such sessions enlightening).

And a word of caution from one of our responding organisations, a branch of the armed forces: check that the women who have "made it" want to be singled out as role models. They told us that many of their senior women did not welcome the internal exposure and external publicity that came with the celebration of their seniority. Respecting women's choices extends to role models too.

3. Work practices

Many companies see the changes that are needed in this area not as a gender initiative but simply as the future of work. The best programmes were looking at the design of jobs, for example by restructuring the work to accommodate people's needs (rather than the traditional approach of people having to fit in with the job structure).

Rethinking job design

But it's still a stretch for many organisations to be creative about job design and accommodate more flexible work patterns. In the UK organisations such as the Timewise Foundation are working with companies to experiment with job design and are getting very good results. Interestingly, where new practises have been embraced there are also more examples of men working flexibly and taking up job-share and part-time arrangements.

Setting up the conversations

One example of redesigning work practices was a team in professional services in the UK undertaking a facilitated process to agree work patterns to cover client needs and the personal commitments of team members. The new arrangements would include work at home protocols and start and finish times, as well as providing cover for late-night client demands which were allocated based on individuals' work preferences and flexibility. So for example, a woman might work her five-day week as four days and a late evening cover worked from home. Another example was work groups agreeing, through a facilitated approach, how to accommodate parental leave returners with different work patterns.

Women returning to work after parental leave told us that organisations seldom realise how important it is to engage the whole team in new work arrangements to ensure they're successful. Many returners had set up the conversations themselves or with help from a parental leave coach. This is an area where structured discussions could help men as well as women adopt work patterns which are more flexible.

Make flexible working normal

Many organisations are trying to make flexible work practices normal: a number told us their policy is that everyone can work flexibly. The default *should* be flexibility, with an obligation to explain why a job needs to be done at set hours or a set location.

Organisations are also encouraging all employees, men and women, to build their work patterns around their needs, rather than set hours. But despite the flexible work policies, and technology which helps people to work outside of the office, the majority of women believe they still pay a penalty for working in a flexible arrangement. And academic research bears this out.

Research participants told us that you can have the best policies in the world but if your manager doesn't really agree with them nothing changes, and you will never be able to meet their expectations. And yet there is strong evidence that allowing people control over their work patterns creates greater job satisfaction and loyalty.

Productive flexibility

For example, staff at travel services provider Ctrip's call centre in China were given the opportunity to volunteer to work from home for nine months. The company set up an experiment: one group worked from home; another group worked in the office. Survey responses and performance data collected after the study showed that, in comparison with the employees who came into the office, the at-home workers were not only happier and less likely to leave but were also more productive.

The other area of focus has been on improving maternity pay and the numbers of women who return to work successfully. Ann Sherry, now Executive Chairman of Australian cruise company Carnival, previously worked for banking group Westpac for 12 years, rising to CEO of Westpac New Zealand. She recounts:

"When I arrived at Westpac, the first thing they wanted was to become an employer of choice. So, I argued the case for paid maternity leave on a rights and fairness basis – as I'd been taught in the public sector, and watched in meetings as everyone's eyes glazed over.

I went back to the drawing board and ran the numbers – and they were compelling. All we had to do was lift the return to work rate by a few percentage points and the program would pay for itself.

That had a domino effect on corporations across Australia because no private organisation had done it at that point. Once we proved it could work, no company could bear to be left behind."

Many of our research participants told us that schemes like parental return coaching and other support had made a noticeable difference in helping women navigate a stressful time with multiple demands when their confidence was often at its lowest. Others said there was still a way to go in their organisation and they were rather baffled as to why it was so hard to persuade managers they could work part time or flexibly when technology made it easy.

Finding technological solutions

Some global organisations were using technology to create international networks, such as pairing up sponsors and keeping women in touch while they were on parental leave as well as using LinkedIn-type applications to help teams around the world access the right skills to help a client or to support each other.

The best companies made these type of applications an integral part of how they tackled their most pressing gender bias issues. In others we found women who were frustrated with waiting for "head office" to take the initiative and had begun doing things for themselves. The women partners in one law firm had created their own app to share their skills and expertise to help them to recommend colleagues to clients.

Creative networking

Other companies were using new software to smooth the transition to new work patterns and were seeing benefits in terms of productivity, job satisfaction and teamwork. These approaches themselves created a greater sense of belonging and were a powerful retention tool.

Software for gender-neutral recruitment

We saw some good examples of organisations using software in recruitment like the Applied software (beapplied.com), which scans draft job advertisements for gender-biased descriptions and presents shortlists of applicants without gender-specific details. It also uses sample work tasks (behavioural tests related to what people must do in the role) as part of the selection process. The idea is to assess as accurately as possible a candidate's *aptitude* for the future job, rather than look at their biographical data to see if they've already done these tasks in the past.

Organisations using this approach told us it was making a huge different to the number of women being considered for traditionally male-dominated roles. It was also raising awareness of the importance of language, and these insights were being applied to other areas like talent reviews. (Similar benefits were being derived from feedback software that we discussed in the chapter on performance evaluations earlier in this half of the book: Chapter 8).

4 The culture

Many companies are focused on inclusive leadership but we believe the "difference that makes a difference" is creating an environment where people don't just feel they're included they feel they *belong*.

Building a sense of belonging

This is more than just warm words. People can be included in a team because their skills are valued or they have done the job somewhere else or they have the right connections for the project.

But *belonging* to an organisation involves not only feeling like we're needed but being recognised for our own distinct qualities and uniqueness. It implies being able to bring the best of ourselves – all of ourselves – to work, whether that's our gender identity, our ethnic background or our wider social conscience. Belonging involves forming lasting, positive relationships with other people, and feeling that we help to shape the corporate culture so that it reflects the values and concerns of people like us.

The distinctions can get confused, of course, because the policies that might build belonging are usually included in what's broadly termed "inclusive" strategies. But by focusing on micro-behaviours and acceptance of what is unique about a person whilst encouraging diverse experience and thinking, it's possible to hold onto this important distinction.

A universal need
A study by Catalyst, the pressure group for greater gender diversity in organisations, found striking similarities across six countries studied (Australia, China, Germany, India, Mexico, and the United States) in how employees describe inclusion; one of the key elements was this deeper sense of belonging. And its important elements were equally true for women and men.

Our research suggests that creating a workplace that is good for everyone is more powerful than a focus on making one disadvantaged group feel they belong. And if you need bottom-line support, research has found a link between belonging and a person's workplace commitment, motivation, pride, energy and engagement.

Creating deep conversations

Creating a sense of belonging is fostered by thoughtful induction, bringing people together where they share information about themselves, and managing attitudes and micro-messages. Some of the mechanisms that were working for companies were women's networks which had a clear role and which provide a safe place for venting and support.

And training leaders and managers in how to manage inclusively is important, including how to have meaningful conversations that really create a sense of connection, helping them to understand why they might react negatively when people put forward different perspectives, and how to manage the discomfort that can arise from working with diverse people.

For example, one research participant told us about an initiative in her company which trained managers to have deep, quality conversations about careers. It was not a gender-specific initiative but women particularly benefited because the more open and in-depth discussions lead to a greater understanding by managers of the challenges women faced, enabled stereotyped assumptions to be tested, and resulting in better career guidance.

Challenging unacceptable behaviour

Our research showed that one of the key issues that needs to be tackled is, in the broadest terms, the *behaviour* allowed in many organisations.

It came as a surprise to us how many of the comments in the Head Heart + Brain survey related to this. 51% of women said they had experienced belittling jokes and behaviour, and 38% had experienced derogatory language directed at themselves or other women. (This was a gender issue: only 19% of men were put down by jokes and behaviour, and a third of the number of men compared with women experienced derogatory language.)

Many senior leaders we spoke to believed there were acceptable standards of language and behaviour in their organisation, but time and again people lower in the ranks would tell us otherwise.

The everyday experiences

What were people noticing? Our research participants' comments ranged from a mid-level woman saying sexual harassment had severely impacted her confidence and undermined her position in the company, to men making fun of the in-house women's network and inventing crude names for it.

One male senior manager in engineering told us behaviour was politically correct in the office, but once people were at lunch, or at the pub, or attending work events, the language and jokes turned against women. A senior woman in a government department said that when she took over a mainly male team she found that sexist language and derogatory jokes were just considered normal. There were also a worrying number of comments about HR departments not taking complaints seriously: brushing them under the carpet or penalising the women who raised the issue.

The power of nudge

Organisations we spoke to are just beginning to experiment with the ideas of "nudge theory" as a way of achieving gender equality. By nudge we mean designing practices and policies to influence attitudes and beliefs so that people will be inclined to do the right thing rather than being compelled to comply with a policy.

Given that we've been trying to tackle gender inequality directly for around 40 years without notable success it may be time to try a subtler approach based on understanding the brain. Numerous studies have shown that a wide range of factors can be influential, including changes in an individual's social environment and expectations.

Both unconscious and conscious beliefs about women are influenced by direct contact with people who don't conform to a stereotype. The woman engineer who's the best in the team, the collaborative banker, the leader who is both demanding and compassionate. People are also "nudged" by the behaviour of senior leaders: by behaviour which belittles women being reprimanded, and inclusive behaviour being praised. So, for example, the manager who stops aggressive language in a meeting with a wink and a smile to the men is signalling it's actually OK. But if he's subsequently passed over for promotion it sends a completely different message to the team.

Subtle encouragement

These practices which signal what is the "right" behaviour encourage individuals to notice and comply with the behaviours which are rewarded in a group. Following the rules of a desirable group is a very strong tendency in human behaviour: it keeps us in the "in-group", and makes us feel part of something beyond ourselves.

Encouraging this kind of socially acceptable behaviour has been very effective in persuading people to use fewer hotel towels, not drop litter and pay their local taxes on time. The desired behaviour needs to be unambiguous and consistent. Behavioural economist Iris Bohnet suggests that the same kind of persuasiveness could be used to encourage action on gender inequality, making it a component in having a good reputation within the organisation, a measure that's considered for promotion, or a behaviour that's publicly rebuked when it's out of order. It's an interesting and untapped area for action, and we need to see more work being done here.

The power of rankings
We can also hope that the soft power of the growing number of published gender equality rankings will prompt organisations to improve their efforts in order to enhance their public image. Leading banker Jayne-Anne Gadhia is not in favour of quotas and imposed targets which she believes can trigger a backlash. She says: "Requiring companies to publish their goals should be the way to hold them to account,"

The UK's recent attempts to require gender pay gap reporting (introduced in 2017) has seen very slow compliance. The widespread tardiness in reporting may be evidence of cynical attempts to get lost in the crowd of late publication and avoid embarrassing public scrutiny. The storm of controversy that surrounded the publication of the BBC's pay imbalance shone a spotlight on the issue, but will not have encouraged other organisations.

Having come up with what they believe are the right initiatives to focus on, Meena and Jay now need to make them happen. They're depending on their understanding of human nature and how our brains work to get buy-in from their peers on the management committee and get their ideas implemented.

Exploring further

Books

What Works, Gender Equality by Design, Iris Bohnet

Articles, blogs and podcasts

Making Good Connections, Susan Vinnicombe, Val Singh and Savita Kumra (Best practice for women's corporate networks.) Opportunity Now, Business in the Community

How Men Can Succeed in the Boardroom and the Bedroom, Sheryl Sandberg and Adam Grant (It's easy to see how women benefit from equality. Men may fear that as women do better, they will do worse. But equality is good for men, too.) New York Times

Closing the Gender Gap Needs Support from the Boss, Sarah Gordon (Three multi-nationals show how it's critical to have corporate leadership for diversity to succeed.) Financial Times

Stop "Fixing" Women and Start Fixing Managers, Avivah Wittenberg-Cox (There is only one key success criteria for gender balancing organisations, and that is leadership.) Harvard Business Review

A Reality Check on Women's Progress in the Workplace, Susan Cramm (Instead of just going along to get along, women need to stand up for what they deserve, to kick up a fuss when they're treated unfairly.) Strategy + Business

Designing a Bias-Free Organisation, Gardiner Morse (Interview with Iris Bohnet about what does and doesn't work in organisations to address gender inequality.) Harvard Business Review

Gender strategy toolkit: A direction for achieving gender equality in your organisation. Workplace Gender Equality Agency, Australian Government

Women in the Workplace 2016 (A comprehensive study of the state of women in corporate America: to give companies the information they need to promote female leadership and foster gender equality in the workplace.) McKinsey & Co and Lean In

Gender at Work is not a Women's Issue, Avivah Wittenberg-Cox. (Is gender a women's issue? Many women still seem to think so.

Which is why many men think so too.) Harvard Business Review

Finally Proof that Managing for the Long Term Pays Off, Dominic Barton, James Manyika and Sarah Keohane Williamson (Long term strategy on diversity and inclusion is needed – and it can pay off.) Harvard Business Review

Videos and webinars

The Power of Belonging, Pat Wadors. Talent Connect, (LinkedIn's Chief Human Resources Officer discusses how creating belonging moments for ourselves and our teams helps attract and inspire top talent.) YouTube (32:57)

The Missing Piece in the Gender Equality Puzzle, Joselyn DiPetta (Since the early days of the gender equality movement, a notion has persisted that the best way to increase rights for women is to focus on women. This strategy is incomplete and leaves out a major factor in achieving equality for women.) TED.com (17:32)

What Works: Gender Equality by Design, Iris Bohnet (De-biasing people's minds has proven to be difficult and expensive. Behavioural design offers a new solution: by de-biasing organisations instead of individuals, we can make changes that have big impacts.) Talks at Google (48:23)

17.
Good ideas aren't enough: how to make change actually happen

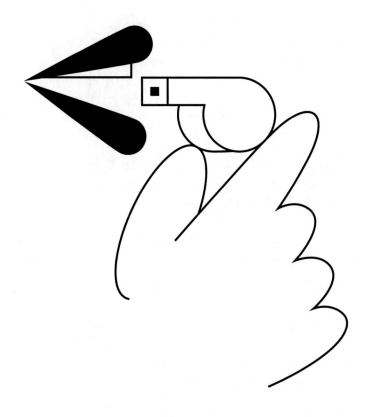

What makes change difficult

Implementing change is hard. Few companies have a successful track record for it, and initiatives in gender are as challenging as every other change programme. Here are some of the challenges you'll be facing, and our experience of what we know works from the Head Heart + Brain research, from our work with clients and using our understanding of neuroscience and other behavioural sciences.

One thing that came through strongly in our research is that the short-term focus of many company leaders makes implementing meaningful initiatives a real challenge. Many leaders told us there's a difference between what they know is needed (which tends to be long-term programmes) and what the organisation can conceive and absorb and therefore what is publicly spoken about (which is often short-term).

People put this down to two things: firstly, the general exhaustion of people in the organisation due to too many change initiatives, combined with a challenging business and economic environment which means people just can't focus on gender issues. Anything that has more than one or two complex elements which need to be changed stands little or no chance of getting traction and buy-in.

Secondly, people are fearful. Initiatives that are challenging, which are long-term and to some extent experimental, create uncertainty. Leadership committees demand precise details which are impossible to provide, and visible changes in very short time-horizons. One leader told us that if she couldn't show progress within one quarter she was unlikely to get buy-in.

It's not a lack of understanding

Our interviewees said this was not about a lack of intellectual understanding: leaders *get* the business case for gender diversity. This was about a physical and mental capacity to change, about a need to increase certainty, finding ways of measuring progress, and getting results which would keep up motivation.

The best organisations manage this by building a strong business case, providing data about where they are on gender diversity and inclusion, and comparing that information with both their competitors' positions (where they can get hold of that information) and the impact on their business (for example, how it might be slowing growth, or costing them more to hire from the market). They also provide regular data on progress which shows what action is needed next.

Time and again we heard that setting out a strategy that was too ambitious, which couldn't point to short-term results or which couldn't provide a picture of what success would look like, just didn't get traction. The organisations which were experiencing the greatest economic instability seemed to suffer most from this short-term focus.

Paint the picture

A significant success factor was the need to provide as much certainty as possible, often where there really was none. This could drive an approach which focused on simple changes involving a limited number of people, or changes which achieved more than one goal. (For example, reverse mentoring of senior leaders might familiarise them with new technology, and also introduce them to the realities for talented women, resulting in "Aha! moments" about how they could support initiatives within the organisation).

These types of multi-outcome initiatives tended to work. Other ways of addressing the need for certainty was for human resources leaders to be skilled at painting a picture of the future. Some senior HR professionals confessed that they couldn't say whether what they were doing would work in a precise way, but by using techniques like sharing stories of successes, and tweaking the picture of what the organisation would look and feel like when the change had been achieved, they helped sceptical and busy leaders make time for the initiatives. This required them to be monitoring results and responding to them and gathering the learning as initiatives rolled out.

The effectiveness of pilots and experiments

One approach which helps new approaches to get off the ground is to run pilots and experiments. Small-scale projects can prove the idea works, increase buy-in, and provide evidence of what can be expected if it's rolled out across the organisation. Those who tried it had good results, and we were surprised that more organisations weren't using this approach. It has the advantage of working with how the brain works: reducing threats and creating rewards in terms of greater certainty, more options, increased reputation for the person introducing a successful pilot (and less embarrassment if it fails) and equity in terms of using limited resources.

For example, one law firm introduced a pilot sponsorship scheme for the next cohort of potential partners. Two board members sponsored each female candidate (the male candidates already had sponsors), received coaching in their role and had time to get to know their partner candidate.

The board members became much more aware of the challenges facing women in the firm, the biases of their colleagues and the untested assumptions being made. The experiment was successful: the candidates were all promoted to partner, but more importantly the sponsors pushed their board colleagues to introduce a more formal sponsorship scheme for future female partner candidates at an earlier stage in their career.

Getting stuck in survival mode

People told us that the busy-ness of modern organisations was a barrier to change. Increased demands, and the impact of always being *on* means that some leaders find it difficult to monitor their behaviour, are inclined to do what they have always done, and are more resistant to change and sceptical about new ideas. These are all behaviours which indicate people are operating in survival mode.

When we're in this mode we've got little spare cognitive capacity and tend to act from our System 1 brain: relying on habit and stereotypes. To counteract this, it was helpful to set out clear behavioural expectations, as well as provide skills training in inclusive behaviours and clear rewards for shifting the dial on diversity in business units. Whilst there was no-one who believed that quotas were a good idea, virtually every company that had made progress had clear diversity *targets* for their leaders, as well as financial rewards linked to achieving them.

Women's programmes make a difference

What also made a difference was development programmes for men and women which had elements for women only, for example a leadership programme where some modules were women-only alongside other modules for both men and women.

The women-only forums provided opportunities for discussing the specific challenges faced by women, while the mixed modules enabled colleagues to work with a diversity of perspectives, learning skills together, appreciating different leadership styles, and developing tolerance for change as well as self-awareness.

Bundle initiatives together

Given the number of change initiatives and people's sheer exhaustion, the more organisations can bundle initiatives together, having one or two that serve more than one purpose, the more likely they are to win support.

The biggest challenges were for global companies trying to initiate change locally and internationally, with projects that sometimes contradict each other. Leaders and sponsors of gender diversity had to work hard to find a common language with colleagues, agree minimum standards and provide flexibility in implementation. In fact, they needed to role-model diversity of approach and an inclusive attitude.

Audit your practices

One useful approach which supplemented data collection and presenting the "story" of diversity and inclusion was to run an audit of practice and process for stereotyped requirements. Audits were generally being used in recruitment but we found few examples in other areas, such as when discussing performance evaluations and calibrating employee ratings. Few organisations we spoke to had a comprehensive approach; most of them focused on where they felt there was the most "noise" or where they could score some easy wins, such as in recruitment.

This can be a good tactic, but it's easy to feel "job done!" The best leaders knew they needed to keep moving forward: once one initiative had proved useful they used that motivation to extend the learning to other areas, such as from external recruitment to internal promotions. Successful organisations kept initiatives linked to the business strategy, kept things simple, used pilots and experiments to prove ideas worked, and looked to design changes that were innovative and solved more than one problem.

Get the ball rolling

The following steps are designed to help you to get the ball rolling on your gender initiative. We're not suggesting you follow them to the letter – just use them as a guide. Use your own judgement about the speed at which you can introduce change and, depending on your organisation's culture and the beliefs of your stakeholders, consider how much of the science it will be useful to reveal.

We often keep the science "behind the curtain" with our clients: the science informs the design and structure of the work we do with them, and it may even be the basis of the policy and practice we develop, but it's not always explicitly mentioned. The change is framed as right for the goals the company is trying to achieve. People have less to think about, and less to worry about.

But some leaders do want to understand the science because they like to know why an approach works: having this evidence helps them accept change. You will know which is the right approach for your organisation.

Our advice is to take one step at a time, review the results and then move on to the next step.

Step 1: Get yourself up to speed on the science of change

Regardless of whether you want to share the scientific evidence around your organisation, you'll want to get yourself up to speed to start with. Our website has lots of resources and we wrote our books so that you can dip into the parts are most relevant to you. You don't have to be an expert: you just need to know enough to understand what will help you.

We recommend you use our success profile of the gender-savvy organisation from the previous chapter to decide where to start. Which of the success factors are you missing? Which might be stagnant? Which will give you a good return on your efforts? If one approach feels high-risk, then think about running a pilot or experiment where you can introduce the ideas in one area and monitor the results.

Step 2: Identify the real issue

First things first: identify the root cause of the issue you're addressing (like losing women in their 30s, or very few women making it beyond middle management grades). We strongly recommend you do some basic research so you know the current state of play with gender in your company: what are the stats, and also what do people *believe*?

A trap that's easy to fall into is solving the *myths* in an organisation: the stories that people tell about why there is a lack of gender equity. For example a myth may be that women don't apply to you, or that they leave because they prefer to stay at home and take care of children. These stories are often based on past truths or historical problems that may not be relevant now.

There will almost certainly be many contributing factors and that can mean you get a bit stuck, perhaps because you have too much data or because you're giving too much weight to the views of one particular set of stakeholders. There are two potential approaches which can help you get the ball rolling.

Get different perspectives
The first is to talk to a number of people who experience the issue from different perspectives, from very senior to the most junior, long-term employees to graduate recruits, employees to suppliers.

Gather your data and then reflect on the patterns you're seeing (the brain is an excellent pattern-recognition machine so you should quickly identify what's recurring, what is only seen by one group of stakeholders, or what you notice but no one else has mentioned). Look also at people's beliefs rather than just the facts: beliefs are what drive behaviour and people will filter the facts to suit their own beliefs.

Find the success stories
The second approach is to pinpoint the teams, departments, leaders and professionals who are working in such a way that they have examples of gender equality practices that work. Understanding the differences that makes a difference to their work can help you transfer those successful practices across the organisation.

Again, talk to a range of successful people, collect the data and analyse. The results will tell you how those departments are successful: the things they do which make the *most* difference. Remember, you don't need to know everything to help others be successful, just the beliefs and behaviours that really matter.

Negative or positive triggers

Which type of diagnosis you do will influence the results you get and will also affect how your stakeholders respond to the feedback. Feedback of negative data will trigger negative emotions like fear, anger, and doubt. They can crank up the "survival energy" and get people moving and action-oriented but they also reduce their creativity, their effectiveness in problem-solving and their willingness to work with other people. And survival energy can quickly dissipate if the issue seems to be fading, which can mean that issues are never fully resolved.

The type of analysis which looks for what's being done *right*, like the Success Profile method, taps into positive emotions which are driven by an urge to connect with others, by trust and an openness to learning. All this sounds good, but it will also feel unfamiliar in many organisations so you'll need to factor that into your decision-making.

Step 3: Planting the seeds and creating insight

Once you have a good idea about the root cause of the problem you want to address (or the success factors of those that are successful *despite* this endemic problem) start talking to the people you'll need to influence and who will need to agree with your approach – your stakeholders. Take it gently, as some of this science contradicts strongly-held views in management, leadership, business and people processes. Such as the belief that emotions make people ineffective, or that you need a burning platform to make change happen.

The brain tends to create a feeling of discomfort when it's faced with new ideas: it will be worth getting people familiar with your proposals before jumping in with both feet. It generally works best to let people have the insight for themselves rather than telling them what they should do or think, so consider the best way to help people get familiar with the science, your data and the potential solutions in your business

Starting small

Could you send them an extract from this book or a link to one of the videos? Or maybe start with one of the shorter articles or blogs on the topic in the *Explore further* section? Once your stakeholders are familiar with the ideas you're introducing, you can start discussing how they might apply in their particular situation. Asking powerful questions can work well here. These are questions that get people thinking differently, shifting their perceptions and beliefs. For example: "What one thing could we change to create greater gender equality?" Or, "If we had no constraints what would we do differently?"

People have more insight when they're in a positive mood, when they're relaxed and when they are not focused on the issue but have done a reasonable amount of prior thinking about it. Too *much* focus tends to mean people get stuck going round and round the same data, thinking in circles. So prime your decision-makers with information or a video-link before a meeting, suggest a break in the midst of a long discussion, or better still come back to the issue the next day when people have slept on it.

The other thing to consider is how your proposals might create a sense of threat or reward: check back to Brain Basics in the Introduction and Chapters 6 and 7 in the other half of this book for some guidance to help you plan your tactics for influencing stakeholders. And don't forget to consider whether people really *want* to solve the issue, or if they have the mind-set that "it's just the way the business works."

Step 4: Planning the solution

Refer to our CORE model in Chapter 1 Brain Basics in the other half of this book to help you anticipate your stakeholders' reactions, identify where you may get resistance and mitigate that threat by creating more "reward" feelings like giving them options or increasing their sense of reputation.

Once people begin to see the value of your gender equality initiative, you should map out how you will move forward and what people will need to be able to do. How big a change is this? Will they need training? Will you need a formal change plan? What do you anticipate the challenges will be, and how can you create a plan to overcome the challenges? How will you measure success and how will you monitor progress in real time to check you're getting the results you want? And what will you do if you face resistance?

Whatever your change plan, getting people involved is what's important: you reduce their sense of threat and harness the collective wisdom of the business.

Step 5: Keep going long enough to establish new ways of working

Many change efforts, be they big or small, fail because the change team stops too soon.

You'll recognise how this also happens with yourself: you think you're in the habit of going to the gym (or meeting with your team, or monitoring their micro-messages...) and then things get tough and you forget to do it. Most of what we do is habit rather than intentional behaviour, because our brains try to operate in the most energy-efficient, habitual way.

Helping people to understand how habits are formed, and supporting and celebrating the new behaviours for long enough for them to take root is what creates real change. No one knows exactly how long it takes to form a habit, but it is longer than a week or even a month. So keep going and give people the support necessary to embed the change.

Jay and Meena have teamed up to work through the Success Profile and look at applying their findings with the organisation.

It's a work in progress but they're excited about the difference they feel they can make. One thing they know is important from the research is to take things step by step, monitoring results, telling the success stories and celebrating their female role models. They're keeping the rest of their leadership team colleagues up to date, and are continually on the look-out for converts who can help them.

We, Jan and Francesca, hope your strategy on gender in the workplace goes well too, whether you're an individual woman using this book to manage your experience, or you're leading a gender equality programme in your organisation. Good luck – and please tell us how you're doing, what's working for you from the book and any new ideas you have found. We look forward to hearing from you at @headheartbrain on Twitter #gendersavvywomen or email us at info@hhab.co.uk

Exploring further

Books

Brain-Savvy Business, 8 Principles from Neuroscience and How to Apply Them, Jan Hills

Pre-suasion: A Revolutionary Way to Influence and Persuade, Robert Cialdini

Influence, The Psychology of Persuasion, Robert Cialdini

The Fear-free Organization: Vital Insights from Neuroscience to

Transform Your Business Culture, Paul Brown and Joan Kingsley

Articles, blogs and podcasts

To Understand Your Company's Gender Imbalance, Make a Graph, Avivah Wittenberg-Cox (How to take a simple look at gender balance in your business.) Harvard Business Review

Corporate Diversity Initiatives Should Include White Men, Avivah Wittenberg-Cox (Good leadership needs to be responsible and accountable for engaging everyone in change.) Harvard Business Review

Videos and webinars

Creating New Habits, Head Heart + Brain (An animation introducing the science of habits with an example to demonstrate how to build a new work habit.) HeadHeartBrain.com (5:13)

CORE: The Model for Change in Business, Head Heart + Brain (A video describing the model and how to use it in change and relationships) HeadHeartBrain.com (6:04)

Building a psychologically safe workplace, Amy Edmondson (The Novartis Professor of Leadership and Management at Harvard Business School, well known for her work on teams. Talks about her research on making team members feel safe.) TED.com (11:26)

Index